S0-BZP-644

A Quick and *Not* Dirty Guide to Business Writing

25 Business and
Public Relations
Documents That
Every Business
Writer Should Know

Charles Marsh

GSP

Gorsuch Scarisbrick, Publishers,
Scottsdale, Arizona

This book is dedicated to my students at the University of Kansas; my business writing mentors, particularly Robert M. Fisher and Gordon Lindsey; and my first editors, Kris, Will, and Gillian.

Publisher:	Gay Pauley
Editor:	A. Colette Kelly
Consulting Editor:	Paul Smeyak
Developmental Editor:	Katie E. Bradford
Production Manager:	Mary B. Cullen
Cover Design:	Don Giannatti
Typesetting:	Ash Street Typecrafters

Gorsuch Scarisbrick, Publishers
8233 Via Paseo del Norte, Suite F-400
Scottsdale, AZ 85258

10 9 8 7 6 5 4 3 2 1

ISBN 0-89787-364-5

Copyright © 1997 by Charles Marsh

All rights reserved. No part of this publication may be reproduced, stored in a retrieval system, or transmitted in any form or by any means, electronic, mechanical, photocopy, recording, or otherwise, without the prior written permission of the publisher.

Printed in the United States of America.

CONTENTS

INTRODUCTION

Business writing helps an organization communicate with groups and individuals essential to the organization's success—everyone from employees to stockholders to the news media. Business documents can take many forms and serve a variety of purposes. For example, a news release about a company's new product and a memo telling employees about new cafeteria hours are both business documents—they just have different purposes.

Good business writing excels in four areas:

- The content focuses on the audience and communicates the document's purpose.
- The organization is logical and clarifies the content.
- The format (appearance and layout) supports the document's purpose and enhances readability.
- The grammar, including spelling and punctuation, is flawless.

A Quick and Not Dirty Guide to Business Writing is short on theory and long on . . . nothing. Its goal is to provide concise, accurate, and reader-friendly guidelines for writing 25 basic business and public relations documents.

The 25 documents are organized into three units: *Internal Documents*, *External Documents*, and *Internal/External Documents*. The numbered documents are easy to find in the book. For each, you'll find clear guidelines for "The Format" and "The Content." In addition, real-world examples illustrate many of the documents.

For more examples, you can turn to Unit Six, *Single-Organization Example Documents*. This unit contains a set of sample documents for the fictitious organization Eclectic Catering and Baked Goods.

Two other units help ensure your success as a business writer. Unit One, *Before You Write*, provides information to help you get started, including tips about the writing process, desktop publishing, using inclusive language, and writing promotional copy. Unit Five, *Writing for the Information Highway*, discusses business documents in the information age, E-mail etiquette, and considerations for creating a web site on the World Wide Web.

This book also has four appendices. *The ACT Agenda* is a system I developed for editing and proofreading business documents. *The Gunning Fog Index* is a time-tested method for assessing the readability of a document. *Writing a Résumé and Cover Letter* offers guidelines and answers frequently asked questions about two documents most of us prepare at least once in our lives. Finally, *Recommended Resources* lists additional sources of information that may be useful to you in your business writing career.

As a good business writer, you're expected to be versatile enough to write many different kinds of documents in clear, vigorous, on-target language. You also may be asked to edit and improve business documents written by others. *A Quick and Not Dirty Guide to Business Writing* will help you successfully respond to these diverse demands.

Good luck! Please call or write to me with your questions or suggestions:

Charles Marsh
Associate Professor
William Allen White School of Journalism and
   Mass Communications
University of Kansas
Lawrence, KS 66045
(913) 864–7642
e-mail: marsh@falcon.cc.ukans.edu

Acknowledgments

I would like to thank the following individuals who reviewed the manuscript for this book and offered valuable recommendations: Anne S. Canfield, Fleishman-Hillard, Inc.; Tom Geddie, ABC; Lynne Sallot, University of Georgia; and Shirley A. Serini, Melvin L. Sharpe, and Gardi Ipema Wilks, Ball State University. I would also like to thank my editors at Gorsuch Scarisbrick, Publishers: Katie Bradford, Mary Cullen, and Colette Kelly.

Thanks to the following individuals and organizations for providing the real-world examples for the book: Jeffrey E. Kobs, Independence Chamber of Commerce; Janet M. Cinelli, *Qcc* Inc.; Caron Van Waart, Bendix/King Radio, Inc.; Amy Hunerberg, Barkley & Evergreen Public Relations; Daniel Hocklander, D. W. Newcomer's Sons; Gordon Lindsey, JCPenney; Duncan Fulton and Karen Quick, Good Fulton & Farrell, Architects; Arizona State Retirement System; *Nation's Cities Weekly; Kansas Alumni; Folio: The Magazine for Magazine Management;* and The University of Kansas.

BEFORE YOU WRITE

The Writing Process

Good writing usually isn't an accident. It's the result of a logical process. Because that process can seem intimidating, some writers prefer to rush in and start writing. That way, they feel that at least they're *doing* something. However, that's like going into battle with no plan and no weapons.

Good writing isn't easy. There's nothing wrong with you if you find it to be hard work. You can make that hard work a little easier by following this standard writing process:

Identify the Need

Samuel Johnson, compiler of the first great English dictionary, said that no one but a blockhead ever wrote—except for money. Let's modify that to "Most people need a good reason to write."

The writing process begins with identifying that good reason. An integral part of identifying your reason involves identifying your audience. For example, do you need to inform employees of a new sick-leave policy? Do you need to thank a loyal client? Do you need to tell the news media (and their audiences) about a significant achievement?

Determine Your Purpose

Be more specific here than simply identifying the need, which you did in step one. What is your exact purpose in communicating with the audience? What is the specific goal of this communication? Ideally, you should be able to answer this question with one clear sentence. For example, "The goal of this memo is to inform department staff that the new sick-leave policy begins May 1."

Then, ask yourself:

- Is your purpose clear and narrowly defined? (If not, perhaps you are facing two or more communication situations and are trying to squeeze them into one.)
- Is the purpose consistent with your organization's goals?
- Does the management of your organization agree that this is the purpose?

Recall your clear, specific purpose as you write your document. Everything in that document should work toward achieving this goal.

Learn About Your Audience

You now know why you're writing, and you have identified your audience. To be truly effective in achieving your purpose, however, you need to learn more about that audience.

What level of language and formality will be most appropriate for the intended audience? How busy is your audience? How long a document will your audience have time to read?

Are your readers mostly within your organization, an internal audience that you know well? Or are they members of an external audience that will be more challenging to study?

Whoever your audience is, consider its members before you write. The most important questions you need to answer are "Why should they care? What is their stake in this situation?"

With answers to those key questions, you can create a document that blends your purpose with your readers' interests.

How do you research an audience? First, gather information that already exists. Ask others in your organization what information they have. When it's appropriate, ask a reference librarian which databases, reference books, and magazine articles might help you understand your audience. As more organizations store information on the Internet and World Wide Web, the information highway is becoming a gold mine of audience information.

If you need more information, consider doing original research, such as in-depth interviews with audience members. Remember that the information you gather from such interviews may not be representative of the entire audience.

You could conduct a scientific survey that *would* be representative of your audience, but such surveys require time, money, equipment, and expertise. For important presentations, consider commissioning such research from an agency that specializes in surveys.

You should become an expert on audiences that you frequently address, such as employees, supplier businesses, or the news media. Constantly improve your knowledge of each audience. Ask its members about their goals. Read the specialized newsletters, magazines, and Internet interest groups that your audiences read. Know who opinion leaders and decision makers are in each audience. Become an expert on what motivates each audience.

Keep up-to-date on current events. Read newspapers. Watch the evening news. Seek out magazines, such as *American Demographics*, and books, such as *Megatrends*, that monitor the beliefs and behaviors of large groups.

Some audiences are gatekeepers for larger audiences. For example, when you send a news release to a newspaper, it must first appeal to an editor before she will prepare the information for the newspaper's readers. Similarly, a newsletter article must first please the newsletter's editor before he will publish it.

Be sure to study what motivates such gatekeeper audiences. Anything that appeals to their readers or listeners probably will appeal to them, but you should still gather gatekeeper information. What deadlines affect such individuals? When is the best time of the day, week, and month to contact them? What kind of information are they seeking for their audience? What is their preferred way of receiving information: fax, E-mail, regular mail, telephone, computer disk, or other method?

Your audience research should generate two types of personal information: demographic and psychographic. Demographic information is "external" information: for example, age, sex, income, and political affiliation. Psychographic information is "internal" information: intangibles such as values and opinions. The line between demographics and psychographics sometimes can be blurry.

Don't be intimidated by doing audience research. It's designed to make your writing job easier, not harder. The bottom line is to identify what motivates your audience. Your goal is to identify each audience's self-interest in each communication situation.

Gather More Information

Now that you thoroughly understand your communication goal as well as the audience you're addressing, it's time to gather information for your document. The information you need generally fits into six categories: who, what, when, where, why, and how.

Apply those six areas to your research-gathering process. Collect information in each relevant area.

You'll find that, often, you've gathered more information than you can include in the document. That's fine; don't try to include it all. Include only information that clearly meets your goal, that addresses the audience's self-interest, and that fits into the space your document allows.

Brainstorm

You probably already have a good idea of what kind of document you'll be writing: a news release, a pitch letter, a magazine story, and so on. Before you make that commitment, stop to consider alternatives. Instead of distributing a memo, should your organization's leader make a speech to employees? Or should there be a memo and a speech? Instead of sending a news release to a journalist, should you send a media kit or a pitch letter?

Ask yourself what document(s) or other forms of communication would most effectively deliver the message.

Organize

You've gathered all the necessary information for a particular document. Now it's time to determine what to include and in what order it will appear.

Many things affect organization: for example, the audience's interests, the type of document you're writing, and the importance of the information. The best general guidelines for good organization are to *be logical* (one part of the document should lead logically to the next) and to *consider your audience* (what organizational scheme will best address its interests?).

Writing an outline, whether it's formal with roman numerals or just notes scribbled on an envelope, will help you refine and remember your document's organization. Don't be surprised if you change or reorganize items as you write. New options may appear as you progress.

For each document discussed in this book, you'll find a traditional, effective organizational scheme.

Write

Welcome to the hardest part of the writing process. Again, writing is tough work for most of us. If you find you just can't get the beginning right, start somewhere else. Your outline allows you to do so. Don't worry about getting the words exactly right in your first draft. At this point, it's more important to express the general ideas.

Revise

One truism of writing says, "Good writing isn't written; it's rewritten." Poet and novelist Robert Graves recommends imagining that your intended reader is looking over your shoulder and saying, "But what does that mean? Can't it be clearer? What's in this for me? What's my reward for reading this part?"

Even if you love your first draft, set it aside for as long as you can. Return to it fresh, and be critical. Approach the document now not as a writer but as a reader. You might try reading what you've written aloud; sometimes this is a good way to catch mistakes or language that doesn't flow well.

Writers who rigorously revise find that, occasionally, they accidentally memorize the document and can revise it as they eat lunch, ride in an elevator, or drive home.

Writing for a Diverse Audience

As we move into the twenty-first century, women and people from ethnic minorities make up a larger proportion of the American workforce. Business writers need to be increasingly sensitive about using inclusive language and avoiding offensive language.

Conscious insensitivity is rarely a problem in business writing. Few business writers deliberately set out to be offensive. Few, if any, use business documents to promote a narrow social agenda that ridicules or excludes particular groups. Unconscious insensitivity, however, can plague well-meaning business writers. Although few of us purposely discriminate, how many of us challenge ourselves to use inclusive language?

Consider the following groups that are and have been the subjects of discrimination:

- women
- members of ethnic and racial minorities
- the physically or mentally disabled
- homosexuals
- the elderly
- members of nonmainstream religions

Other groups, of course, could be named. Make it your goal to identify and eliminate any biases you may unwittingly harbor toward any group. These biases might reveal themselves in your business documents, resulting in ineffective communication.

Edit

Editing can be thought of as the last fine-tuning of your document. Sometimes, editing is just an extension of revision. Ask yourself where the document can be more clear. Can the sentences be shorter without losing meaning or becoming too abrupt?

Instead of that adjective-noun combination, is there a more precise noun? Instead of that adverb-verb combination, is there a more precise verb?

Are you using forms of "*to be*" too often? Are more exciting verbs possible? Is the grammar correct? Does the opening in some way invite the reader to keep reading? Is the document complete? Does it answer the relevant parts of who, what, when, where, why, and how?

Is your best material buried? Should you reorganize now that you better understand the document?

INCLUSIVE LANGUAGE

- Balance personal pronouns. For unnamed, generic individuals such as *supervisor* or *senator*, don't always use *he*, and don't always use *she*. At the same time, watch out for illogical shifts. A hypothetical supervisor shouldn't change gender within a paragraph.

- Use caution with words that describe particular relationships: *your wife, your husband, your boyfriend, your girlfriend, your parents, your children*. For example, female readers generally are excluded by *your wife*, and male readers generally are by *your husband*.

- Avoid potentially sexist words, such as *postman, fireman*, and *chairman*. Seek alternatives, such as *postal worker, fire fighter*, and *chair* or a nonsexist synonym that avoids the word *chair* altogether.

- Avoid words that unnecessarily specify a gender: for example, *waiter/waitress, executor/executrix*, and *bachelor/bachelorette*. When possible, use the unmarked word (the word without the feminine suffixes *-ess*, *-ix*, and *-ette*) for both males and females.

- If you're going to identify an individual as a member of a minority group or any group that is or has been the subject of discrimination, ask yourself these questions:

  1. Do you really need to identify this individual as a member of that group? In other words, is such identification important to the message you want to convey? Often it is not.

  2. If it is logical and appropriate, have you also identified everyone else in the document as a member of a group?

  3. If such identification is essential, are you using an appropriate term? Selecting the appropriate term can be challenging. Should you use *black* or *African American? Senior citizens* or *elderly? American Indian* or *Native American? Gay* or *homosexual? Hispanic* or *Latino? Moslem* or *Muslim? Disabled, handicapped*, or *impaired?*

     The answers vary. If you must identify an individual as a member of a particular group, references such as the *Associated Press Stylebook* can

continued

help. You also can ask associates and acquaintances. You won't be able to please everyone.

4. The following information from the Bureau of Labor Statistics may help. In May 1995, a bureau survey of almost 60,000 households gathered the following information on preferred racial and ethnic terminology:

   – Blacks prefer *black* (44.15 percent) to *African American* (28.07 percent) and *Afro-American* (12.12 percent).

   – Hispanics prefer *Hispanic* (57.88 percent) to *of Spanish origin* (12.34 percent) and *Latino* (11.74 percent).

   – American Indians prefer *American Indian* (49.76 percent) to *Native American* (37.35 percent).

   – Multiracial individuals prefer *multiracial* (28.42 percent) to *mixed race* (16.02 percent).

- In documents that cite individuals, draw upon diverse sources. In many organizations, it's easy to rely on a steady stream of white, Anglo-Saxon males in their forties and fifties. Surely not all qualified sources are members of this group. Try to add diversity to your citations. In doing so, you are more likely to appeal to the diverse workforce.

- Know the dates of major religious holidays.

- Finally, avoid being overzealous in your quest for inclusiveness. Not every group in society can be represented in every document.

Are you following your organization's style and format for documents? Remember that organizations may vary in their guidelines for writing documents.

See Appendix A, The ACT Agenda, for more specific editing guidelines.

Proofread

This is best done backwards, one sentence at a time (see Appendix A, The ACT Agenda). The reversal breaks up the flow of the document and helps you focus on each sentence to see what you actually wrote instead of what you meant to write.

Check every fact and every possible misspelling. Check grammar one more time.

Many writers find this to be the most tedious part of the writing process—and many have saved their careers by spotting and correcting errors at this point.

Seek Approval

It's now time to pass the document to someone else—often your boss—for review. This step can be painful, but it's essential. You're so close to the document now that being objective is difficult.

Never distribute a document without a second opinion and formal approval.

Distribute the Document

You now must send your document out into the world. You may not be responsible for distribution, but you have a major investment in the document's success. Be sure you know where it's going and how it's getting there. And then be sure that it got there.

Evaluate

Did the document succeed? It succeeded if you achieved your purpose. Did the news release lead to a published story? Did the newsletter article increase applications for the training program? Did follow-up questions to the speech show that the audience understood?

Did your document influence its audience's behavior in the intended way? If so, why? If not, why not? If possible and appropriate, ask recipients of the document.

Was the distribution efficient? Why or why not?

Because business writers generally are so busy, evaluation is one of the most overlooked steps of the writing process. But the evaluation of past documents leads to future successes.

Ten Tips for Writing Better Sentences

1. *Challenge "to be" verbs.*

   Challenge every appearance of *am, is, are, was, were, be, being, been,* and every other form of the *to be* infinitive. Sometimes a *to be* verb best suits the needs of the sentence—but often you can find a stronger, more evocative verb.

ORIGINAL	REVISION
He *will be* a good communicator.	He *will communicate* well.
We *are inviting* you . . .	We *invite* you. . . .

2. *Use active voice.*

   In active voice, the subject of the sentence does the action. In passive voice, the subject receives the action.

PASSIVE VOICE	ACTIVE VOICE
Our profits *were affected.*	A sales slump *affected* our profits.

   Passive voice is grammatically correct—and it's the right choice when the action is more important than the action's doer (EXAMPLE: She was fired.). But passive voice can seem timid, and it requires a *to be* verb. In contrast, active voice is confident and concise.

3. *Challenge modifiers.*

   Modifiers (adjectives and adverbs) can strengthen a sentence by sharpening your meaning. But sometimes they prop up weak words, especially nouns, verbs, and adjectives. A precise, well-chosen word needs no modification.

ORIGINAL	REVISION
We are *very happy.*	We are *ecstatic.*
Quickly take your report to the client.	*Rush* your report to the client.
He is *rather tired.*	He is *tired.*
Please deliver the package to our *headquarters building.*	Please deliver the package to our *headquarters.*

4. *Challenge long words.*

   If a long word or phrase is the best choice, use it. Otherwise, use a shorter option.

ORIGINAL	REVISION
utilize	use
revenue-enhancement measure	tax

continued

5. *Challenge prepositional phrases.*

Avoid a string of prepositional phrases:

ORIGINAL	*REVISION*
We will meet *on* Thursday *in* Centerville *at* the Lancaster Hotel *on* McDaniel Street *near* the harbor.	We will meet Thursday *at* Centerville's Lancaster Hotel, 1423 McDaniel Street.

Some prepositional phrases can be tightened into adjectives:

ORIGINAL	*REVISION*
I will present the report in the meeting on Thursday.	I will present the report in Thursday's meeting.

6. *Challenge long sentences.*

How long should a sentence be? Long enough to make its point clearly and gracefully—and no longer. Watch for sentences that are more than 25 words; realize that some good sentences will exceed that length. As discussed above, eliminate *to be* verbs and tighten prepositional phrases when possible.

7. *Avoid overused expressions.*

"Bizspeak" expressions such as "It has come to my attention" and "I regret to inform you" are so common that they sound insincere. Also, clichés such as "He's a fish out of water" are so common that they don't create the engaging image they once did.

8. *Avoid placing important words or phrases in the middle.*

The beginning of a sentence breaks a silence and calls attention to itself. The last words of a sentence echo into a brief silence and gain emphasis. The middle of a sentence generally draws the least attention. The importance of sentence openings and closings can be different, however, in scripts for radio and television. For guidance on such scripts, see Documents 14–16.

9. *Keep the focus on the reader.*

Tell readers what *they* want to know—not just what *you* want them to know. Keep the focus on how they benefit from reading your document.

10. *Read your sentences aloud.*

Or at least whisper them quietly to yourself. That's the surest way to check for effective sentence rhythm.

Appendix B, the Gunning Fog Index, can help you write effective sentences.

Ethics and Business Writing

A code of ethics establishes guidelines for behavior. Such codes go beyond legal codes and into the sometimes unclear world of what's right and what's wrong. Something legal, for example, isn't always ethical.

Knowing the right, honorable course of action often is easy. The difficulty can arise in performing the right, honorable action. Sometimes, the unethical alternative can appear easier and less challenging and therefore more appealing. For example, announcing and taking responsibility for a serious error—when that error is your own—can be difficult.

The origins of the word *ethics* suggest the challenges of achieving ethical behavior. The Greek origin is *ethos*, or *character*. But the earlier, Indo-European root of the word, according to the *American Heritage Dictionary*, is *s(w)e*—which means that related words include *secret, sober, solitary, sullen, desolate, idiot*, and even *suicide*.

Why do business writers need to practice good ethics?

Good ethics is good business. Study after study shows that organizations that strive to do the right thing reap economic rewards. Customers prefer their products or services, and these organizations attract and retain the best employees. Other studies show that ethical managers flourish in their careers.

There are other reasons for practicing good ethics. Greek dramatists believed that we all eventually face a moment of *anagnorisis*—a moment of piercing self-recognition, of moving from ignorance about ourselves to complete self-knowledge. Most of us, in facing such a moment, would like to see a life well-spent, one built upon honorable, productive relationships with others.

Where do business writers find ethics guidelines?

Ethics codes—written and unwritten—exist at many levels:

- societal (for example, the Ten Commandments)
- professional (for example, the ethics codes of the Public Relations

Society of America and the International Association of Business Communicators)

- organizational (an organization's written ethics code)
- personal (an individual's ethics code)

The ethics code that will matter most to you is your personal code. As a writer, you know that putting your thoughts on paper stimulates thinking and prompts precision, so consider writing a personal ethics code. Draw upon societal, professional, and organizational ethics codes to create your own.

The best times to create and revise your code are when you are *not* facing an ethics crisis. In the depths of such a crisis, you'll need the clear, well-reasoned standards you established when you were free from doubts and fears. A crisis, of course, can prompt clarification and expansion of your personal ethics code.

What might be included in a business writer's personal ethics code?

A worthy goal for any business writer is to create documents that are honest, complete, timely, and disseminated, and that seek honorable relationships between the sender and the recipients.

Honest Documents

- Context can affect honesty. For example, if you note that a production quota was met for the first time, you might also need to note that the quota had been reduced dramatically so that it could be met.
- Hard truths can sometimes hurt. Be diplomatic. Put yourself in the place of those affected by those truths.
- For legal and other reasons, documents cannot always contain every detail about every matter. But your documents should include accurate details put into the proper context.

Complete Documents

- As noted above, you must sometimes withhold information. Justifications for withholding information include legal restrictions, individual rights to privacy, and loss of competitive advantage. Information should not be withheld simply because its dissemination could make life unpleasant for the sender or because withholding it would help preserve the sender's power.
- *Complete* is a relative term. Recipients should be given all the information they need. Most don't want to be buried in an avalanche of minutiae. If there's any doubt about what information a recipient needs, offer the information that you believe best

fits that description—and then offer to provide more upon request.

Timely Documents

- Important information should be disseminated quickly. This is particularly true in times of crisis for the sender or recipient or both.

Disseminated Documents

- The goal of dissemination should be to reach every individual who needs to see that document. Meeting that goal requires using the communications channels preferred by the recipients—which may not necessarily be those you prefer.

Documents That Build Honorable Relationships

- As a business writer, your mission is to protect and promote your organization by nurturing important relationships. Occasionally, the temptation to pursue an unethical course can be conquered by considering the long-term impact on a relationship. For example, when an honest communicator conveys bad news, the recipient may be disappointed but often will also respect the courage and integrity of the communicator. In an honorable relationship, that respect will remain long after the disappointment has faded.

What are some of the toughest ethics problems for business writers?

No-Win Situations

For many business writers, the toughest ethics problems involve dilemmas—that is, situations in which every possible course of action involves disadvantages.

For example, what should you do when a supervisor you respect asks you to withhold important information that should be in a document? Disobeying him could be disastrous for your relationship and your career. Obeying him could violate your personal ethics code.

What can you do? Ideally, you've helped create an environment in which such ethics dilemmas can openly and diplomatically be discussed. If not, you might wish to consider the advice of the Public Relations Society of America. That organization's code of ethics states that members must resign from any organization that would force them to act unethically.

A third option is described in this book's section on writing a memorandum (see Document 17). Write the supervisor a memo describing the action he has asked you to take. Then ask, in the memorandum, if you have understood his instructions. As he sees his own unethical request in writing and realizes that a paper trail is about to begin, he might reverse his decision. Of course, such a memo might weaken your relationship with the supervisor.

Heavy Workload

Good business writers often are overworked. Although there can be financial and other professional rewards for that burden, overwork can be a source of unethical communication. Overworked business writers may not have the time to seek all the relevant facts, confirm their accuracy, place them in context, and quickly disseminate them to all appropriate recipients.

If such a business writer bills her time to either internal or external clients, this problem is avoidable. Her organization should hire more good business writers, and fair estimates of expected charges should be given to all clients.

A business writer confronted with this problem could decide to accept fewer clients, if she is able to make this decision. If she works for someone else, she could discuss with a supervisor the possibility of hiring additional staff. She might point out that a larger staff would be able to handle the workload with greater efficiency and fewer errors.

Rules of the Game

Business writing can be a noble, rewarding activity—especially if you follow these rules of the game:

1. *Do the right thing.*

   Never lie or distort the truth in a business document. Never use someone else's work without permission. Generally, when you lose your credibility, it's gone forever. History shows that, in the long run, being honest and compassionate is good for business. Take that long view. Do the right thing.

2. *Protect and promote your organization.*

   This the basic duty of the business writer. In everything you do for your organization—especially creating documents—your goal should be protection and promotion. Even in something as routine as a memo announcing new parking-garage policies, you can promote your organization by being sensitive about the impact of the change.

3. *Before writing, always consider audience and purpose.*

   Who is your audience—exactly? What characteristics does it have? What is its stake in the situation your document addresses? And what are you trying to tell that audience—exactly? In other words, know precisely whom you're addressing, what motivates them in this situation, and what your message is.

4. *Don't write something that you don't understand.*

   Ask dumb questions—many, if necessary. It's better than making dumb mistakes. Most business professionals love to discuss what they do (and they enjoy showing off their knowledge), so they won't mind the questions.

5. *Communicate as business documents progress.*

   Let others, especially bosses and clients, know how a document is progressing, especially if difficulties occur. Don't hide problems. Announce them as soon as possible, but also announce potential solutions.

6. *Produce an error-free document.*

   The ACT Agenda, in Appendix A of this book, will help you cover the nine areas of a document that must be reviewed in the editing and proofreading stages.

Desktop Publishing for Business Writers

Many business writers today must also be designers. Using desktop publishing software, they design brochures, newsletters, and other documents that contain the text they've written.

Desktop publishing, however, is an imprecise term. *Publishing* actually refers to the dissemination of information. When we use the term *desktop publishing*, most of us mean desktop design—that is, designing a brochure, a newsletter, or another document on our computer screens.

This short section won't make you a desktop publishing expert. To gain that expertise, you can enroll in classes, read instruction manuals, study successful designs, consult professionals, and simply practice with the programs.

Nor will expertise with desktop publishing software make you a designer. Such programs are tools. Knowledge of good design comes first.

This section will help you ask some questions that can lead to good design.

Before selecting a design for your document, ask yourself these questions:

What questions regarding the document are foremost in your readers' minds and how can design help immediately answer those questions?

EXAMPLE

Suppose you're crediting a brochure for a local politician. Your research has shown that potential voters have concerns regarding her advanced age and uncertainties about where she stands on a proposed tax increase for schools.

You might establish her vigor with a photograph showing her engaged in a clean-up of city parks. And her stance on the school-tax issue could be stated clearly in a "breakout" quotation—that is, a quotation set in large type.

With such design, the readers' foremost questions are answered even before they get to your text.

How can design help spotlight key elements of your message?

EXAMPLE

Just as readers have key questions, you have key points you want to convey. In the political brochure described above, the politician may want to stress that she's accepting no money from political action committees. Could a large, bold headline introduce a short section on that topic? Could a logo be designed to emphasize that point—perhaps a crossed-out dollar sign? In short, how can design help make that point before you describe it in a short paragraph?

How can design make your document easier to read?

EXAMPLE

The average age of the population in the United States is increasing. With that increase comes a decrease in the ability to read small type. Enlarging the type size of a newsletter—or simply increasing the space between the lines—can seem to be an insignificant design decision, but it can be a big hit with many readers. The generous use of "white space"—that is, areas with no text or design whatsoever—boosts readability.

How can design help grab and retain your readers' attention?

EXAMPLE

An important but superficially boring business report might be energized with a dynamic logo and vibrant colors on the cover. That logo might be carried throughout the report, even in a reduced size next to page numbers.

How can design help give a long document continuity and coherence?

EXAMPLE

In the business report described above, continuing a reduced logo near each page number can help give the report coherence. Consistency in colors, type fonts, and type sizes can do the same.

DESIGN

- Analyze successful (and unsuccessful) brochures, newsletters, and other documents designed by others. Be specific about what works and what doesn't. Don't simply duplicate someone else's successful design. Merge your own good ideas with your new knowledge.

- Use contrast to lead the reader's eyes. Ideally, not every element in your design will be the same size or the same color. Your reader's eyes will be drawn first to the larger elements and the most vibrant colors.

    Using too much contrast, however, can lead you into an error that some professionals call "circus design." Circus design uses too many type sizes, too many fonts, and too many colors; your document ends up looking like a garish circus poster. For a moment, such design can grab attention, but with every element screaming for attention, the reader's eyes don't know where to begin.

- Don't fill every square millimeter of your document with text, photographs, headlines, charts, logos, enlarged quotations, or swatches of color. Leave some white space. Allow both the document and your reader to breathe.

- Avoid postage-stamp-sized photographs of intricate scenes. Spare the eyes of your older readers.

- Don't dramatically change the design of regularly written documents such as news releases and newsletters. Strong, consistent design helps the reader to remember the identity of your organization and its publications.

- Seek training in both the principles and the tools of design from experienced, award-winning professionals.

- Finally, don't be so dazzled by creating a design that you undernourish the text. A badly designed but well-written document can still fulfill its goals. A well-designed but poorly written document usually cannot.

Rhetoric and Business Writing

The Art of Dramatic, Graceful, Persuasive, and Memorable Writing

Rhetoric is the art and science of persuasion. Its main tool is language.

The key to successful rhetoric? An understanding of what motivates your audience and a willingness to write several drafts of a document.

Described below are rhetorical devices that can work particularly well in business writing. Related devices are grouped together under headings such as "The Power of Silence." For some techniques, the actual Greek or Latin name is noted.

Use these devices to clarify meaning and heighten drama—not to hide or obscure the facts.

The Power of Silence

Closing Emphasis

- At the end of a sentence, paragraph, or document
- Use the silence that follows the end of a sentence, paragraph, or document. The closing words echo into that silence and gain emphasis.

  EXAMPLE

  Our goal is clear: improved profits.

Opening Emphasis

- At the beginning of a sentence, paragraph, or article
- Use the silence that comes before a sentence. The words that break that silence will call attention to themselves and gain emphasis.

·EXAMPLE
Improved profits—that is our goal.

Dramatic Pause

- Created by a colon or dash that generally follows a complete sentence
- In the example above, note how *improved profits* gets both opening and closing emphasis. It breaks a brief silence and then echoes into another silence.

EXAMPLE
We must be clear on one key point: failure is not an option.

The Power of Rhythm

Blunt Sentence or Blunt Sentence Fragment (Brevitas)

- Used to emphasize a blunt idea, especially when this short passage is surrounded by longer sentences. Its difference—its brevity—makes it stand out.
- Several blunt sentences in a row create a choppy rhythm, building tension and drama.

EXAMPLE
We'll never quit. Not now. Not ever.

One-Sentence (or Sentence-Fragment) Paragraph

- Used to emphasize a blunt idea, especially when this paragraph is surrounded by multi-sentence paragraphs

EXAMPLE
When Jane Smith graduated from Harvard, people asked if she was satisfied. When she landed her first job at XYZ Corporation, they asked if she was fulfilled. Last year, when she became XYZ's chief executive officer, they asked if she had attained her dream. And her answer was always the same.
    No.

Opening Repetition (Anaphora)

- Used at the beginning of several consecutive sentences. Repetition of opening words establishes a pattern, and that pattern calls attention not only to the repeated words in each phrase but also to the new words that break the pattern in each phrase. Note the slight shift from "must" to "will" in the example—and note how that shift is highlighted with a blunt, one-sentence paragraph.

EXAMPLE

Increased productivity must be our new motto. Increased productivity must motivate our every action. Increased productivity must haunt our dreams.

Increased productivity will ensure our success.

Closing Repetition (Antistrophe)

- Used at the end of several consecutive sentences. Repetition of the closing words emphasizes those words. Like opening repetition, closing repetition highlights differences as well as similarities. In the example, the people who will win begin to stand out as much as the word *win*.

EXAMPLE

Our stockholders will win. Our employees will win. And, best of all, our families will win.

Triplets (Groups of Three Words)

- Can be placed anywhere in the sentence. Triplets tend to be pleasing to the ear. Be sure there's a logical order to the three items. Place the most powerful word last in the phrase. This will ensure effective closing emphasis.

EXAMPLE

"Friends, Romans, countrymen" or "Unwept, unhonored, and unsung"

The Power of Sound

Repetition of an Opening Sound (Alliteration)

- Used wisely and sparingly, can call attention to key words. The example is intentionally excessive so that it will be memorable.

EXAMPLE

Constant Concern for Customers Can Create Considerable Cash.

Pleasing Sounds (Euphony)

- A succession of long, open vowels and soft consonants. Euphony helps convey your meaning when you describe a pleasing, soothing scene.

EXAMPLE

His slow, soft voice soothed the weary troops.

Harsh Sounds (Cacophony)

- A succession of short, flat, closed vowels and hard consonants. Cacophony helps convey your meaning when you describe a harsh, unpleasant scene.

  EXAMPLE
  The spotlight's harsh glare ignited the garish colors.

Rhyme

- Can be annoyingly cute if misused. But rhyme also can be used to make a phrase memorable. It sometimes works well in feature article headlines and subheadlines.

  EXAMPLE
  Jennifer Johnson is bright, right, and ready to fight.

The Power of Sentence Structure

Subordination

- A useful way to convey bad news. The bad news is placed in an opening dependent clause (which can't stand alone as a complete sentence). That dependent clause is weaker than the following independent clause, which contains the good news. Also note how placing that dependent clause at the beginning pushes the bad news into the middle of the sentence, or the point of least emphasis.

  EXAMPLE
  Although profits are down, morale remains high.

Parenthetical Expressions

- Can be used to bury bad news in the middle, the least emphatic part of any sentence, paragraph, or article

  EXAMPLE
  Our profits, which are down, are only part of the picture.

Passive Voice

- Can be used to downplay the doer of the action because the doer of the action is not specified. Note that passive voice is useful for conveying bad news.

  EXAMPLE
  He was fired. (Rather than "Mary Jones fired him.")

Emphatic Sentence Fragment(s)

- Works best when most of the text is in complete sentences. That way, the fragment or fragments stand out and attract attention.
- A fragment must clearly be intentional. It shouldn't appear to be a flawed sentence.

EXAMPLE

We will never retreat. Not today. Not tomorrow. Never.

Non-Traditional Word Order (Hyperbaton)

- Can call attention to a key passage

EXAMPLE

We promised to advance, and advance we will.

Reversed Word Order (Antimetabole)

- A statement that establishes a word order and then reverses it for a new meaning
- Because it's clever, antimetabole can make an idea memorable.

EXAMPLES

It isn't just; it just is.

When customers win, we win customers.

Linked Opposites (Antithesis)

- A balanced sentence in which the meaning shifts 180 degrees or in which opposites are compared
- Antithesis is used to highlight and contrast opposing ideas.

EXAMPLE

While our competitors were content with yesterday's products, we sought tomorrow's dreams.

The Power Beyond the Written Word

Connotation

- The "aura" that surrounds a word

EXAMPLE

initiative rather than *proposal*

Euphemism

- A diplomatic alternative to a harsh word or phrase

EXAMPLE
challenge or *opportunity* rather than *problem*

Graceful Repetition of a Key Word

- Can help establish a theme. The document's audience may consciously or unconsciously begin to associate that word with your message.

  EXAMPLE
  She is a leader: A leader in the workplace, a leader in her church, and a leader in the community. (The repeated word needn't be packed into only one or two sentences. It can be distributed gracefully throughout the document.)

Allusion

- An indirect reference to a fairly well-known historical or literary figure or work. The feelings evoked by that figure or work carry over to your document. You don't need to attribute the allusion to the particular literary work.

  EXAMPLE
  Using the words *liberty and justice* might evoke feelings related to "The Pledge of Allegiance." Those patriotic feelings might then be associated with the message you're sending.

The Power of Imagery

Simile

- A comparison of dissimilar things using either *like* or *as*
- A good simile can give readers a specific, memorable image, which may help them remember a key point. The same is true for metaphors, personification, and hyperbole.

  EXAMPLE
  Good communications are like a garden.

Metaphor

- A comparison of dissimilar things without using *like* or *as*

  EXAMPLE
  Good communications are a garden.

Personification

- Giving human qualities to an inanimate object

EXAMPLE

Our company is reaching for the stars.

Exaggeration (Hyperbole)

- Overstating for dramatic impact

EXAMPLE

Our company has moved mountains to achieve record profits.

Use of Specific Details

- Used for clarification and entertainment because specifics are more visual and entertaining than generalities
- Paint word pictures for your audience with specific details: sights, sounds, smells, or the feel or taste of something.

Promotional Writing

Promotional writing isn't a particular document. It can be found in effective memos, productive business letters, and stirring company announcements. Promotional writing, instead, is a style of writing. The Latin roots of *promote* mean "to move forward." In promotional writing, you're often trying to move an idea forward—to a point at which the audience accepts it.

The key to successful promotional writing? Identifying and addressing the audience's self-interest in each particular communication situation.

Remember the Basics

As always, begin by considering two things:

1. Your audience: Focus on audience members' self-interests in this situation.
2. Your purpose: Be clear and succinct in defining it.

Be Persuasive

Promotion is often based on persuasion—that is, promotional writing has a style that motivates a reader to do something. The Greek philosopher Aristotle identified three types of persuasion:

- Appeals to the intellect
- Appeals to the emotions (Note: Appeals to guilt, fear, and other negative emotions can backfire.)
- Appeals to a sense of ethics (Note: Most important in this appeal is the ethical value of who you are. In other words, your reputation precedes you. Aristotle said that the most powerful persuasive tool is not logic but the known character of the person or organization using the logic.)

Some forms of persuasion combine two or all of these approaches. Given your knowledge of the audience, decide which appeal or combination of appeals will work best.

Use the AIDA acronym discussed in Document 23, The Brochure. AIDA stands for Attention, Interest, Desire, and Action.

Use the rhetorical techniques listed in "Rhetoric and Business Writing" in the previous section of Unit 1. Recall that rhetoric is the art and science of persuasion.

Be Brief

Promotional writing often has a few seconds, at most, to hook its readers and keep them reading.

- As quickly as possible, let the audience know how it will benefit by reading the document.
- Remember a maxim of advertising: big ideas in small words.
- Remember an important acronym in good communication: KISS (*Keep It Simple, Stupid*—or, more diplomatically, *Keep It Short and Simple*).
- In tight writing, pay particular attention to your verbs. Interesting, appropriate verbs will punch up almost any kind of writing.

Know What Not to Say

Sometimes what isn't said can be as powerful as what is said.

- Respect the value of connotation (see "Rhetoric and Business Writing").
- If the subject to be promoted is controversial, consider acknowledging and countering opposing views. This should be done carefully, of course—but leaving it undone can damage the credibility of your writing.

   One effective way to counter the opposition is to refute it in a way that doesn't openly acknowledge that it exists. For example, if you're trying to attract potential employees to a seminar about your department store and a rumor holds that your store is out of step with current fashions, stress your fashion victories. Don't acknowledge the fact that you're presenting one side of a dispute. In other words, don't try to make a positive point by denying a negative point. Avoid the "I am not a crook" strategy.

Make an Impact with Graphics

Combine words with visuals when appropriate. Studies show that after three days, we retain only 10 percent of what we hear and only 35 percent of what we see. But we retain 65 percent of what we both see and hear. Often, members of your audience aren't *hearing* your message—they are reading it, which can be even more effective. But good graphics can still make your written words more memorable.

EXTERNAL DOCUMENTS

External documents leave the hallowed halls of your organization. They are directed to groups or individuals who, though not part of your organization, can influence your organization's success.

THE BUSINESS LETTER

Document 1 The Good-News Letter
Document 2 The Bad-News Letter
Document 3 The Sales Letter
Document 4 The Request Letter

THE NEWS RELEASE

Document 5 The Announcement
Document 6 The Feature
Document 7 The Hybrid
Document 8 The Short Teaser
Document 9 The Media Advisory
Document 10 The Pitch Letter

THE MEDIA KIT

Document 11 The Backgrounder
Document 12 The Fact Sheet
Document 13 The Photo-Opportunity Sheet

WRITING FOR BROADCAST MEDIA

Document 14 The Broadcast News Release
Document 15 The Radio Public Service
    Announcement
Document 16 The Video Treatment

The Business Letter

The Purpose

The business letter is one of the most common forms of business communication. There are several different kinds of business letters. Among the most common are:

- the good-news letter
- the bad-news letter
- the sales letter
- the request letter
- the pitch letter (This letter is discussed later as Document 10. Although it is formatted as a business letter, it is used in place of a news release.)

This section presents the standard format for such business letters. It also includes content suggestions that apply to most business letters.

The Format

With rare exceptions, keep the letter to one page.

Whenever possible, use your organization's stationery. Use your organization's stationery for the envelope as well.

Use the proper headings, generally aligned along the left margin. (See box on p. 31.)

Avoid an inadvertently sexist greeting. For example, if you're writing to Lynn Jones, is that individual a man or a woman? Is it "Dear Mr. Jones" or "Dear Ms. Jones"?

Single-space the recipient information and the paragraphs of the letter.

Double-space between:

- the date and the recipient information
- the recipient information and the "Dear Mr. or Ms."
- the "Dear Mr. or Ms." and the text of the letter
- the paragraphs of the letter (don't indent the paragraphs)
- the text of the letter and the "Sincerely"
- your typed title at the bottom and any extra notes, such as "cc" or "encl."

Your Organization's Letterhead Here

Today's date

Mr. or Ms. Recipient's First and Last Names
Recipient's Title
Recipient's Organization
Organization's Street Address
City, State (no comma) ZIP

Dear Mr. or Ms. Last Name:

Thank you very much for . . .

*A comma can be friendlier than a colon, but it's also less formal. Address the recipient by last name—unless you know her well. If you address her by first name only, you may wish to use a comma instead of a colon to keep the informality consistent. If you address her by first name only, be sure you sign **your** first name only above your typed full name at the bottom of the letter.*

- When you're writing a business letter that isn't on your organization's letterhead—such as a letter to accompany a résumé—your headings, above the recipient's name and address, should look like this:

Your Street Name
Your City, State (no comma) ZIP
Today's Date

 Note that your name doesn't go here. It goes at the bottom.

Type "Sincerely" at the bottom left. ("Sincerely," because it is traditional, is almost always the best sign-off. It is courteous and conservative. A less traditional closing might draw attention from your name and title.)

After "Sincerely," skip down four to six spaces (enough space for a *legible* signature). Type your name. Under your name, type your title. Don't type your organization's name here; it's already on the stationery.

Above your typed name, remember to *sign the letter.*

Notes at the bottom are also placed on the left side:

- "cc" means you've sent a copy to the person you name.
     EXAMPLE: cc: Mary Jones
   "cc" stands for "carbon copy," which is obsolete, so often you'll just see "c" for "copy."
- "encl." means that some other document has accompanied your letter. Check to be sure you've enclosed it.

A sample closing for business letters is shown on p. 32.

Again, thank you very much for your time and effort. I look forward to meeting you next Friday.

Sincerely,

Your signature

Your Typed Name
Your Title

cc: Mary Jones { *This is optional.*

QUICK TIPS

- Within the first few sentences of most business letters, the recipient should know why she is reading the letter. That is, she should know why you're writing to her. *Sales letters and bad-news letters can be exceptions to this guideline.*
- The closing of the letter often specifies or suggests what the next action should be. When appropriate, the closing should say what you'll do next or what you hope the recipient will do next, or both.
- As always, realize the value of courtesy. Opening and closing with a thank-you, whenever appropriate, is both good manners and good business.
- Sound like an intelligent, sincere human being, not a machine. Avoid clichés such as "It has come to my attention" and "I regret to inform you." They're so overused that they sound insincere.
- Sign legibly.

The Good-News Letter   1

The Purpose

A good-news letter conveys information that will please the recipient: a job offer, a refund, an award, and so on.

The key to successful good-news letters? Get to the good news quickly.

The Format

Follow the general guidelines for business letters on pp. 30–32.

The Content

The good-news letter has three or four parts that usually will translate into three or four paragraphs.

Deliver the Good News

Open positively. Deliver the good news immediately. Or, if the recipient first wrote you with a request, you can thank her for contacting you. Then announce the good news: for example, a refund. If the good news involves an award, a promotion, or the like, express congratulations.

If your good-news letter is in response to a complaint, begin, as noted above, by thanking the individual for writing. Then, in one sentence, be understanding but don't apologize in a way that accepts blame. For example, you can write, "I regret that you're unhappy with the quality of our service." After the apology, briefly announce the good news. (Everything mentioned in this paragraph could be included in a three- or four-sentence opening paragraph.)

Explain the Details

In a new paragraph, explain the details of the good news. For example, will you be issuing a refund check? When will it be mailed? Are you inviting the recipient to an awards banquet? When and where will it be? In this section, inform the recipient of any details he should know to take advantage of the good news. (If this information includes a request to contact you, you may wish to save that until the closing of the letter.)

QUICK TIPS

- Keep the focus on the recipient. Don't write at length about you and your organization unless the recipient needs or desires that information.
- If you're responding to a negative situation with good news, empathize. How would you feel if the roles were reversed?
- When responding to a negative situation, don't disparage your organization. (It's tempting to deflect the recipient's anger by agreeing with him—that is, to share the recipient's anger so that it's not directed at you personally.)
- When responding to a complaint, know what you can offer and what you can't. If you don't know, ask the appropriate person in your organization.
- Remember that you represent your organization. Be courteous—even if you haven't received such treatment from the recipient.
- Make no commitment on behalf of your organization that it can't or won't keep.

Document 1, Good-News Letter: *In this example, the first paragraph closes with the good news. The good news thus gains emphasis by "echoing" into a brief silence.*

Independence
Chamber
of Commerce

April 10, 1997

Mr. John Calver
President
Calver Communications
10200 West 75th Street, #108
Shawnee Mission, KS 66204-2242

Dear John:

Thank you for your theme and logo development bid for Santa-Cali-Gon Days --
Independence's annual Labor Day weekend celebration. After reviewing the top five
proposals during its April meeting, the fair board voted unanimously to accept your bid.

The enclosed letter of agreement outlines the key points of your proposal, as well as the
stipulations required by the Chamber of Commerce. Please read, sign and return the letter
at your earliest convenience. To complete all elements of the campaign on time, we need
rough logo sketches and theme ideas prior to the board's May 16 meeting.

I'm extremely excited to work with you on this challenging project. Your background
and marketing expertise will be a valuable resource for the Chamber of Commerce. I will
be your primary contact and board liaison during the course of the campaign. I look
forward to meeting with you to plan our next step.

I will call you on Wednesday morning of next week to discuss a time and place for our
initial meeting. If you have any questions or concerns beforehand, please feel free to call
me at 252-4745.

Sincerely,

Jeffrey E. Kobs
Communications & Small Business Director

encl.

ACCREDITED

P.O. Box 1077, 129 W. Lexington, Independence, Missouri 64051 • Telephone (816) 252-4745 • Fax (816) 252-4917

Say What It Means to You (Optional)

If appropriate, in a new paragraph you may include the impact of the good news on you or your organization or both. For example, if your letter offers the recipient a job, this paragraph could mention how delighted you are to offer this job and how you look forward to working together.

End the Letter, Perhaps with Instructions

In your final paragraph, be courteous and positive. Include the details about how the recipient can contact you if necessary. Consider specifying what the next action should be. If you are responding to a situation brought to your attention by the addressee, you may thank the writer again for contacting and informing you. If congratulations are in order, you may express them once again. Include a standard "Sincerely" sign-off.

2 The Bad-News Letter

The Purpose

Bad-news letters tell their recipients something they don't want to hear: no refund, the impossibility of a donation to charity, and so on.

> The key to successful bad-news letters? Explain the reason(s) for the bad news before you announce the bad news.

The Format

Follow the general guidelines for the business letter on pp. 30–32.

The Content

The bad-news letter has five parts that often will translate into three paragraphs.

Begin Courteously but Neutrally

Thank the recipient for contacting you, if that's appropriate. If possible, find some common ground to comment on. Be polite, but not *so* enthusiastic or upbeat that it sounds like a good-news letter.

If you're responding to a complaint, you can apologize here, if that's appropriate. Again, be careful not to apologize in a way that accepts responsibility for a bad situation. You can say, "We too regret this unfortunate situation." Such wording doesn't accept responsibility; it's more an expression of sympathy.

Explain the Reason(s) for the Bad News

In a new paragraph, logically, neutrally, and briefly explain the reason(s) for the bad news that you're about to deliver. This is important: You deliver the explanation for the bad news before you deliver the bad news. When the recipient receives the bad news a few moments later, he will understand, ideally, the logic of your decision.

For example, before telling a job applicant that you can't hire her, first explain that there are no positions open for someone with her qualifications. Deliver the explanation before you deliver the bad news.

The first sentence of this new paragraph is an important "bridge." It should gracefully move the letter from the neutral introduction to the coming explanation of the bad news. Avoid a sudden, startling change of tone.

Deliver the Bad News

In the same paragraph as the explanation, state the bad news clearly and concisely—in one sentence, whenever possible. Avoid setting this bad-news sentence off as a one-sentence paragraph; one-sentence paragraphs get extra emphasis, and you don't want that. If possible, put the bad news in the middle of a paragraph, which is a point of low emphasis. The bad news won't get the extra emphasis that paragraph openings and closings get.

Write Something Neutral or Positive After the Bad News

As noted above, don't let the bad-news sentence close the paragraph—don't let it "echo" into the silence that follows a paragraph. Close the paragraph with something neutral or positive.

For example, if you're turning down a job applicant, write that you'll keep her résumé on file for one year and will contact her if any suitable jobs open.

Note that the above three sections ideally go in the same paragraph.

QUICK TIPS

- In the bad-news explanation and the bad-news sentence, avoid whenever possible the words *you* and *your*. In the bad-news sentence, also avoid any form of *I* and *we*. Avoiding those words can help you keep the focus firmly on the situation, not on the people, although this isn't always possible.

- Some writers can be long-winded in a bad-news letter, attempting to hide the bad news in an avalanche of words. Don't be blunt to the point of rudeness, but be concise.

- Don't let personal feelings, such as anger or sympathy, excessively influence your letter. Your job is to protect and promote your organization. You might hurt it by being overly emotional in your letter.

- As noted in the discussion of the good-news letter, don't disparage your organization. (It's tempting to defuse an angry recipient by agreeing with him, but you shouldn't write something like "I agree that we didn't perform very well.")

- Avoid stock phrases such as "It has come to my attention" and "I regret to inform you." They're so overused that they sound insincere.

- This bad-news organizational scheme—first the explanation, then the main point—can be used in memos and speeches as well.

Document 2, Bad-News Letter: *In this example, the bad news is de-emphasized by its position in the middle of a paragraph—and that paragraph is in the middle of the letter. Middles lack the emphasis that openings and closings attract.*

*Q*cc, Incorporated

April 11, 1996

Mr. Mark Johnson
Donations Coordinator
United Human League
130 57th Street
New York, NY 10009

Dear Mr. Johnson:

Thank you for your information on the United Human League and the work it does to protect human rights throughout the world. As I explained when we spoke, *Q*cc selects its charitable organizations each Spring for its next fiscal year. The company's charitable donation committee considered more than 100 charitable organizations this year covering various themes such as human rights, education and the environment.

Each year, *Q*cc's charitable donation committee chooses a theme and provides donations to charities that meet that theme. Although we believe that the United Human League is a worthy organization, it does not fit with the theme *Q*cc has chosen for next year. For fiscal year 1997, *Q*cc has selected education as its theme and will be providing sizeable donations to the National Education Foundation, the Inner-City School Association and Education First.

Thank you again for providing me information on the United Human League. *Q*cc will begin its fiscal year 1998 charitable organization search in mid-March of 1997. I will keep your information in our donation files for further consideration at that time.

Sincerely,

Janet M. Cinelli
Chairperson -- 1997 Charitable Donations Committee

8829 Bond Street
Overland Park, KS 66214
(913) 492-1230 • FAX: (913) 492-1684

Close Positively or Neutrally

In a new paragraph, close positively, if possible. If not, close neutrally. Do not mention the bad news in this closing paragraph. (Avoid writing, "Again, I regret . . ." You will just be highlighting the bad news by repeating it.) If it's appropriate to mention a continuation of the relationship between you and the recipient, do so. Include a standard "Sincerely" sign-off.

Exceptions to the Standard Organization

When the bad news refers to an unacceptable situation that needs immediate improvement, you may want to consider a different organizational scheme, especially when recipients are aware of the situation:

- In the first paragraph, immediately announce the bad news. A very brief explanation may come before this.
- In a new paragraph or paragraphs, discuss in detail what's being done to improve the situation.
- In the next paragraph, announce the communications step to follow. Should the recipient contact you? Will you phone her? Will you write additional letters to keep the recipient informed?
- Close with a standard "Sincerely" sign-off.

In a time of crisis, you might send such a letter to members of audiences whose support you need.

3 The Sales Letter

The Purpose

Sales letters attempt to persuade the recipient to purchase your goods or services, or, perhaps, to donate to a charity.

Sales letters are challenging. Often, they're mass produced, which can (but ideally shouldn't) prevent you from including knowledge of individual recipients. Sales letters can use a variety of organizational schemes and are generally written by professionals with years of experience. Often, they're longer than one page.

> The key to successful sales letters? Open by filling the recipient with a sense of need or desire—and then return to that scenario in the closing.

The Format

Follow the general guidelines for business letters, found on pp. 30–32.

The Content

Create a Sense of Need or Desire

Don't start by asking for the sale. Instead, create a sense of need or desire within the recipient. Often, this means creating a scenario that presents a familiar problem or desire to the recipient. Don't mention or hint at your product yet. The goal of this section is to remind the recipient that something in his life needs to be better. In a short sales letter, this section generally is only one paragraph. Note that the sales letter doesn't follow the tradition of using the first paragraph to tell the recipient why he's reading the letter.

Present Your Product as the Solution

In a new paragraph, satisfy the recipient by noting a solution to his problem: your product. Be specific about how your product solves the problem and improves the recipient's life. Be clear, not vague, about your product's characteristics. In a short sales letter, this section can be more than one paragraph if necessary.

Ask for the Sale

In a new paragraph, ask for the sale. Or demand it: "Order yours today. It's easy. Just . . ." Be sure to give all the details of how the recipient can acquire the product. In a short sales letter, this section usually is one paragraph.

Document 3, Sales Letter: In this example, the letter opens and closes by focusing on a potential problem in the recipient's life. It contains two sales requests: the subtle "Your adoption of the revised edition" and the stronger "Call me today to request a complimentary copy...."

PROSPECT PRESS

The Full Service Publisher

8233 Via Paseo del Norte, Suite E-400 • Scottsdale, Arizona 85258

February 10, 1997

Mr. Frank Solomon
Director
Solomon School of Real Estate
31 Delwood Avenue
Champaign, IL 61820

Dear Mr. Solomon:

Are your students reading a textbook that is outdated? As you may know, the Illinois legislature recently made major changes to laws that affect the real estate business. But did you know that as a result, your students may be learning incorrect information from the textbook they are using?

Prospect Press is pleased to announce the release of a textbook that will meet your students' need for the latest information, including current Illinois real estate law. The Revised Edition of *Illinois Real Estate Principles & Practices,* by Palmer & Joseph, will be available for examination on March 10, 1997.

The enclosed flier briefly summarizes the most significant changes in the text. The Table of Contents on the reverse side gives you a more detailed look at what this new edition has to offer you and your students.

Your adoption of the revised edition will be accompanied by an instructor's manual, transparencies, and a computerized testbank that includes Illinois-specific questions. New questions have been added to test students' knowledge of the new legislation.

"Preparing for a Real Estate Salesperson Examination," the interactive software tutorial, completes the student learning package. It's designed to accompany the student through the Palmer & Joseph text, chapter by chapter, with special emphasis on the most challenging topics. It is extremely user-friendly and offers the student the kind of help that only a tutor could provide!

Don't let your students go into their license exam with outdated knowledge. Take advantage of this opportunity to adopt the most current and accurate integrated Illinois text on the market.

Call me today to request a complimentary copy for consideration for your sales transaction course. The call is toll-free: 1–800–555–8398. I look forward to talking with you soon.

Sincerely,

Eric Patterson

Eric Patterson
Sales Manager

encl.

Re-evoke the Sense of Need or Desire and Again Ask for the Sale

In case the recipient has become too relaxed, in a new, final paragraph return to the theme you developed in the first paragraph: Something is missing in his life. After briefly re-evoking that sense of need, tell him to get your product today. Include a standard "Sincerely" sign-off.

QUICK TIPS

- Focus on the recipient's self-interest. He doesn't care what you think about the product. He wants to know what it can do for him.
- Avoid excessively negative or morbid scenarios in your first and last paragraphs.
- Some sales letters, especially those in direct-mail solicitations containing brochures and other items, are longer than one page. The theory is that if the recipient clearly sees how he benefits from your product, he'll continue to read for that length.
- Consider using some of the promotional strategies discussed in "Rhetoric and Business Writing" and "Promotional Writing" in Unit One of this book.

The Request Letter 4

The Purpose

Request letters ask someone outside your organization for something you need: information, a special proclamation, a hard-to-find object, and so forth. Request letters can use different organizational schemes, depending on their purpose. If the letter is a request for funds (a fund-raising letter), the organizational scheme for the sales letter (Document 3) can work well. If the letter is a request for anything else, the organizational scheme in this section works well.

The key to successful request letters? Ask promptly, explain your request, and close by noting future action.

The Format

Follow the general guidelines for business letters, found on pp. 30–32.

The Content

The request letter typically includes the following components:

First Paragraph.   Briefly identify yourself and make the request. Getting right to the point is courteous because you're not wasting the recipient's time.

Second Paragraph.   Explain the request. For example, why do you need the information? Why do you deserve a refund? Be specific but concise.

Third Paragraph.   Identify any special needs: deadlines, specific questions you need answered, and so on.

Fourth Paragraph.   Explain what action you will take next—or what action you hope the recipient will now take. Thank the recipient. Include a standard "Sincerely" sign-off.

Quick Tip

- Large businesses will use their own envelopes to reply to you—if a letter is the proper response. But small organizations or private individuals might appreciate a self-addressed, stamped envelope enclosed with your letter.

Document 4, The Request Letter: In this example, the request gains emphasis through its placement at the end of the first paragraph. It "echoes" into a brief silence. Note the same technique in the good-news letter on p. 35.

BK RADIO, Inc.
2901 Lakeview Road, Suite 100
Lawrence, Kansas 66049
(913) 842-0402
Fax: (913) 841-0287

February 11, 1997

Ms. Amy Mauch
Trade Show Coordinator
Firehouse Expo
445 Broad Hollow Road, Suite 21
Melville, NY 11747

Dear Ms. Mauch:

I recently saw an advertisement for the Firehouse Expo in Firehouse magazine. I am interested in possibly attending the 1998 Firehouse Expo. Could you please send me an exhibitor's prospectus?

My company manufactures two-way mobile and portable radios specifically for the public safety market, and I think this show would be a nice addition to our schedule.

I am currently planning our 1998 trade show schedule and would appreciate any information you could send me. Thank you for your help, and I look forward to attending the 1998 Firehouse Expo. If you have any questions, I can be reached at 800-555-0947 ext. 6834.

Sincerely,

Caron Van Waart

Caron Van Waart
Advertising and Public Relations Manager

The News Release

The Purpose

A news release is a document that conveys newsworthy information about your organization to the news media. Most often, it is written in a "ready-to-publish" format.

The news release is often called the press release—which is now inappropriate because many of us get most of our news from television and radio.

Still, news releases have a bias toward print media. That is, most are prepared, basically, for a newspaper. Other media then edit the release for their particular needs.

In general, there are three styles for standard news releases:

- the announcement
- the feature
- the hybrid

Three other documents are similar to news releases. Unlike news releases, they are not in "ready-to-publish" form:

- short teasers
- the media advisory
- the pitch letter

These six documents are described in Documents 5–10.

The key to successful news releases? A news release must contain only newsworthy information. It should not be a thinly disguised advertisement for your organization. Good news releases have a local angle. They focus on what the news means to a particular medium's audience.

The Format

Send the release on your organization's stationery—ideally, stationery designed specifically for a news release. Generally, use letterhead stationery only for the first page. (Don't switch to different paper quality for page two, however.) In mass mailings, it's all right to use photocopies of letterhead stationery, but if the budget permits, use originals.

Heading

Begin the release with a heading that includes "FOR IMMEDIATE RELEASE," the composition date, a contact person (and her title), and a phone number. If the stationery doesn't label this as a news release, type "News Release" in big, bold letters. A byline here is optional.

The heading should be single-spaced.

Leave about two inches between the heading and the headline for an editor's notes. For example:

Organization Letterhead

News Release

FOR IMMEDIATE RELEASE
Aug. 1, 1997

STORY BY: Miranda Gomez

For more information, contact:
Catherine Jones
Account Executive
(555) 123-4567

Red Cross schedules downtown blood drive

The Headline

Your headline should be in newspaper style.

Boldface the headline. Capitalize the first word and any names (of people, buildings, organizations, and so on). Lowercase all other words, just as most newspapers do.

The Text

Double-space the text of the release; editors need room to edit.

The text of a news release should be as long as necessary to tell the story concisely. The entire release should rarely be more than two pages—one front and one back, or two separate pages. Make it shorter, if possible.

Consider using legal-size paper (11" x 14") for a long one-page release. Don't do two-page releases on legal-size paper. (Some editors don't like legal-size paper because it doesn't fit well into standard file folders.)

Page Numbers, Slugs, and Similar Items

If the release is more than one page, type "-more-" or "-over-" at the bottom of each appropriate page (it's all right to print on both sides of the paper). Beginning with page two, place a condensed version of the release's headline (called a "slug") and the page number in the upper-right corner. At the end of the release, put "-30-" or "end" or "# # #." Staple the pages of the release together. Never trust a paper clip.

The Content

Focus on your audience: a journalist who seeks newsworthy information for her audience. What kind of information is newsworthy?

- Information that affects members of a news medium's audience.
- Information that is unusual or exceptional.
- Information about a well-known individual or organization.

The Headline

Most newspaper headlines are, roughly, complete sentences, written in the present tense (or sometimes in the future tense if you refer to something that hasn't happened yet). The headline summarizes the story's main point. Whenever gracefully and logically possible, mention your organization's name or product in the headline.

The Dateline

Begin the text with a dateline and a dash (for example, "DALLAS—").

Datelines give the location of the story; the writer, ideally, should be in the datelined city.

The Text

Build a strong hook into the first paragraph. Usually, that hook is concise, specific, newsworthy information with a clear local angle. The first paragraph (the lead) must induce the reader to continue reading. Ask yourself the traditional who, what, when, where, why, and how questions. Use the key information from those areas in your lead paragraph.

The rest of the news release typically is structured as an inverted pyramid, with less important information toward the end of the news release. Consider including a pertinent, attention-grabbing quotation from a spokesperson of your organization. Such quotations can enliven a news release.

For more specific content guidelines, see Documents 5–10.

Optional Notes to the Editor

If some information, such as the spelling of a name, is unusual, include a single-spaced "Note to the Editor" after the "-30-" to inform editors that your information is correct. This is not necessary for routine information.

Distribution and Follow-Up

Send all news releases to specific people by name and title. Find out who the appropriate editors are at each medium. *Bacon's Media Directories* and *Working Press of the Nation Media Directories* can be a big help.

If the release announces an event, be sure that newspapers, radio stations, and television stations receive it about 10 days before the event. Magazines may need much longer. Six months isn't too early for some magazines. If your release is highly newsworthy, some magazines may wish to include a related story in their editorial calendars and use that story to attract advertising.

Consider paying a distribution service, such as PR Newswire or Business Wire, to distribute the release for you. For a price, such services electronically transmit your release directly to newsroom computers. New studies are showing that editors prefer to receive news releases electronically, via newswire services, fax machines, or E-mail. If you're going to use E-mail, write to the E-mail address first, requesting permission to send news releases.

QUICK TIPS

- Avoid the words *today*, *yesterday*, and *tomorrow*. Unless you actually have the date in the dateline, editors will have to change that word. Your *today* will be days later by the time your release is published or broadcast. How should you specify dates? Study the styles of the news media you're targeting.
- Don't waste words. Write clearly and to the point.
- In all news releases, remember the value of the local angle. Ask yourself why your news will appeal to the audience of each medium to which you send your release.
- In the announcement, feature, and hybrid styles, don't be too promotional. You, as the writer, must be completely objective. Don't include unattributed opinions (your opinions) about your organization's excellence. If the release is just a thinly disguised ad for your organization, its chances of being published in any form are remote. Strive for an objective voice that appeals to editors.
- Be certain that your managers and your clients review and approve the news release before it is distributed. After reviewing their comments or suggested revisions, you may need to remind them that a news release must be an objective, unbiased news story.
- Many editors resent embargoed releases—that is, releases that aren't for immediate publication. With an embargoed release, you ask the editor to hold the information until a specified release date. Don't make a practice of asking editors to hold newsworthy stories.
- If possible and when appropriate, include a "gimme": a sample of the product, a photograph with a caption, a Rolodex card, and so on. Such items attract an editor's attention (see "The Media Kit" in Unit Two).

A continuing debate in public relations concerns follow-up calls—that is, telephoning journalists to ensure that they received the news releases and to offer help. Most journalists resent such calls. If your release does its job and has a good local angle, journalists will call you if they need more information. If you must call regarding a release of crucial importance, be polite. Remember: Journalists are under no obligation to use your story. Often, you won't get through to the journalist to whom you sent the release. When that's the case, leave a message that specifies why you're calling. One more call back is fine, but don't make a nuisance of yourself.

Send only one release to each news medium. A newspaper, for example, generally won't want two reporters working on the same story. If you have two completely different angles on the same story, you might send two different releases, but even then, in a closing "Note to the Editor," you should inform each journalist of the other news release.

The Announcement   5

The Purpose

The announcement is by far the most common type of news release. Use the announcement for standard "hard-news" stories—for example, the announcement of a new chief executive officer.

The Format

Follow the general guidelines for news releases on pp. 46–51.

The Content

The announcement imitates a straightforward newspaper story. The lead (that is, the opening paragraph) covers the most important aspects of who, what, when, where, why, and how. The story follows the inverted pyramid structure; in other words, the information becomes progressively less important. The least important (but still

Document 5, Announcement News Release: This announcement release reads as if a reporter, not a business writer, wrote it. The only opinion in the release—the comparison of the award to a Pulitzer Prize—is attributed to a credible source.

The University of Kansas

William Allen White School of Journalism
and Mass Communications

News Release

FOR IMMEDIATE RELEASE
April 15, 1996

FOR MORE INFORMATION, CONTACT:
Mike Kautsch
Professor and Dean
(913) 864-4755

University of Kansas students win national journalism award

LAWRENCE, Kan. -- Students at the William Allen White School of Journalism and Mass Communications at the University of Kansas have won first place in the Print Division of the national Hearst Journalism Awards. The school receives $10,000 for its first-place finish.

"The Hearst Journalism Awards often are called the Pulitzer Prizes of college journalism," said Mike Kautsch, professor and dean of the William Allen White School of Journalism and Mass Communications. "We're pleased that our students compare so favorably at the national level."

The school will receive its first-place medallion and cash award May 20, 1996, at the Hearst Journalism Awards ceremony in San Francisco.

Students in journalism schools throughout the nation compete in the yearlong Hearst competition in such categories as in-depth writing, sports writing and opinion writing. The school that accumulates the most points throughout the year wins the competition. This year, 101 accredited undergraduate schools of journalism participated in the Hearst Journalism Awards.

Award-winning students from the University of Kansas were:

-more-

KU Journalism - 2

- Jenni Carlson, first in sports writing.
- Colleen McCain, third in spot news and ninth in in-depth writing.
- Matt Hood, third in feature writing.
- Novelda Summers, fourth in profile writing and eighth in in-depth writing.
- Christoph Fuhrmans, fourth in sports writing and 14th in spot news.
- Virginia Margheim, seventh in profile writing.
- Rufus Coleman, 17th in opinion writing.

"These students have brought more than honor to the school," said Rick Musser, Clyde M. Reed Teaching Professor of Journalism at the University of Kansas and coordinator of the school's participation in the competition. "In the past three years, our scholarship program has received more than $50,000 in Hearst award money."

The William Randolph Hearst Foundation fully funds and administers the Hearst Journalism Awards.

The William Allen White School of Journalism and Mass Communications at the University of Kansas is a fully accredited school of journalism. It offers bachelor of science and master of science degrees. In 1995, the school finished second in the Hearst competition. In 1994, it finished first.

-30-

newsworthy) information comes last in an announcement news release.

The release usually is written in past tense. If, in your lead, you need to establish that this was the very recent past, you can use present-perfect tense. For example: "The XYZ Corp. has announced the hiring of Mary Jones as its new corporate treasurer."

An announcement release often includes relevant quotations from appropriate sources, such as members of your organization's management. Trade magazines, business journals, and small newspapers sometimes reprint announcement news releases verbatim. Other media may turn them into brief announcements or use them to generate longer stories. (Remember: The media may ignore the news release altogether, especially if it's poorly written, too promotional, or has no local angle.)

6 The Feature

The Purpose

The feature news release is less common than the announcement (see Document 5). Use the feature for "softer" human interest stories.

The Format

Follow the general guidelines for news releases on pp. 46–51.

The Content

The feature is "softer" than the "hard-news" tone of the announcement. Some feature news releases offer entertaining human interest stories, such as an officer of your organization who makes a special effort to hire the homeless. Other feature releases attempt a less direct view of your news by focusing on topics ostensibly bigger than your organization.

For example, Hallmark Cards writes feature news releases on the traditions of important holidays, such as Halloween. In addressing this interesting topic, the release uses Hallmark experts and information for evidence, thereby bringing notice and credibility to that company. Some feature releases strengthen their credibility by including information from nonemployee, noncompetitive sources to round out the article.

Avoid the temptation to include unattributed opinions in a feature news release. Like all news releases, it must be objective and unbiased.

Feature news releases don't have traditional news leads. Instead, the lead attempts to spark the reader's interest with a question, an anecdote, an image, or a similar device.

Feature news releases use storytelling skills, so they're not inverted pyramids, as are announcement news releases. The most dramatic paragraph in a feature news release might be the final paragraph.

Since feature news releases aren't nearly as newsworthy as announcement releases, they're rarely as successful. If your organization has an interesting story, but it's not a good, hard-news story, a pitch letter (see Document 10) may be your best option.

A more extensive discussion of feature stories can be found in Document 21, The Newsletter/Magazine Story.

The Hybrid 7

The Purpose

The hybrid news release can be ideal for a "hard-news" story that has a whimsical or human interest angle. For example: a medical center's free health fair for senior citizens.

The Format

Follow the general guidelines for news releases on pp. 46–51.

The Content

The hybrid combines the announcement style and feature style of news releases. The hybrid has a feature-like lead, designed to attract the reader's attention. Then it moves to an announcement style, delivering the facts in inverted pyramid form. Unlike the feature, its information becomes progressively less important.

8 The Short Teaser

The Purpose

Short teasers can offer several story suggestions in one concise document. Teasers aren't meant to be published verbatim; instead, they're designed to catch a journalist's fancy, to induce her to contact you for more information about a potential article. Teasers work well when you want to publicize a large event with several possible stories—and when there's enough time for a reporter to develop a story.

The Format

Teasers can be in the format of a pitch letter (see Document 10), but more often they are a series of bulleted (•), single-spaced, related story ideas under the headings of a traditional news release (p. 47).

The Content

Each story idea receives roughly one paragraph. If appropriate, a different contact person can be listed for each bulleted idea.

An introductory paragraph below the headline but above the bulleted ideas can help explain this document to journalists.

The Media Advisory 9

The Purpose

A media advisory is a who, what, when, where, why, and how outline of a newsworthy story. It is appropriate in two situations:

- The news it outlines is extremely timely and you need to get the information to the news media as quickly as possible.
- You are sending the advisory as a reminder to media editors and reporters of a previous, important news release.

A media advisory usually is faxed or electronically transmitted to newsrooms.

The key to successful media advisories? They should contain only very timely news, and a reporter should be able to write a short, complete news item from the media advisory alone.

The Format

The heading of a media advisory is the same as that of a news release (p. 47), except that you label it a media advisory. That distinction is important because a media advisory conveys a sense of urgency.

Media advisories are short and to the point—one page, if possible. They are not meant for publication in their present format. Thus, they are single-spaced, with double-spacing between paragraphs.

After the heading, most media advisories arrange their information something like this:

What: Gov. Jane Smith will tour the Midtown Recycling Center.

The tour will be private, but reporters may join. The governor will accept questions regarding her visit and her recycling policies after the tour.

Who: Mike Jones, Midtown Recycling Center founder and president, will conduct the tour for the governor. Midtown Mayor Lynn Johnson will join them.

When: Saturday, Sept. 14
3–4 p.m.

Where: Midtown Recycling Center
3956 Main St.
Midtown

Why: "I'm visiting the Midtown Recycling Center because it's a model facility for the rest of the state. It's the perfect example of my administration's recycling policies."

—Gov. Jane Smith

Note how similar this is to a fact sheet (see Document 12). Despite the similarity, fact sheets and media advisories are used for different purposes. A fact sheet usually accompanies a news release in a media kit. A media advisory is usually used for late-breaking stories that don't allow time for the writing of a full news release.

The Content

As mentioned above, the traditional media advisory is a who, what, when, where, why, and how outline of the essential facts. It begins with the most important area (often the *what*) and then moves to the second most important area (often the *who*) and so on. There's no attempt at a story form—but a reporter should be able to write a short news story from the media advisory alone; it should be that complete.

Document 9, Media Advisory: This advisory updates the photo-opportunity sheet on p. 71. A follow-up telephone call to area photographers could help advise them of the time change.

The University of Kansas

William Allen White School of Journalism
and Mass Communications

Media Advisory

FOR IMMEDIATE RELEASE
April 22, 1996

FOR MORE INFORMATION, CONTACT:
Mike Kautsch
Professor and Dean
(913) 864-4755

TIME CHANGED FOR FRIDAY, APRIL 26, JOURNALISM AWARDS CEREMONY/PHOTO OPPORTUNITY

Students at the William Allen White School of Journalism and Mass Communications at the University of Kansas have won first place in the Print Division of the national Hearst Journalism Awards. The school receives $10,000 for its first-place finish.

The Hearst Journalism Awards often are called the Pulitzer Prizes of college journalism.

*The prize-winning students will be honored in a brief ceremony Friday, April 26. **The ceremony will begin at 3 p.m.** This is a half-hour later than the time specified in a Photo Opportunity sheet dated April 15.*

What: Awards ceremony for KU journalism students who placed in the national Hearst Journalism Awards.

Who: • Jenni Carlson, first in sports writing.
• Colleen McCain, third in spot news and ninth in in-depth writing.
• Matt Hood, third in feature writing.
• Novelda Summers, fourth in profile writing and eighth in in-depth writing.
• Christoph Fuhrmans, fourth in sports writing and 14th in spot news.
• Virginia Margheim, seventh in profile writing.
• Rufus Coleman, 17th in opinion writing.

When: Friday, April 26. **NEW TIME: 3 p.m.**

Where: Woodruff Auditorium, Kansas Union
University of Kansas
Lawrence, Kan.

-30-

200 Stauffer—Flint Hall · Lawrence, Kansas 66045-2350 · (913) 864-4755

> # QUICK TIP
>
> - Because media advisories are comparatively rare and highly newsworthy, you may telephone recipients to ensure that they received the document and to see if you can provide additional information. Avoid this procedure with standard news releases.

10 The Pitch Letter

The Purpose

A pitch letter is a replacement for a feature news release. It is a letter, addressed by name to a journalist, that pitches a "soft-news" story idea. It promotes a story that isn't earthshaking news but still is of local interest and, therefore, is newsworthy. Your goal is to get a reporter to write the story.

Should you use a pitch letter instead of a feature news release? Ask journalists which they prefer. Before deciding to send a pitch letter, consider these facts:

- Pitch letters generally take less time to read than feature news releases. Busy journalists will appreciate that.
- In a pitch letter, as opposed to a feature news release, the story isn't yet written—so a reporter can feel a stronger sense of ownership of the story.
- Small newspapers and trade magazines that publish news releases verbatim may prefer feature news releases to pitch letters; they may not have the staff to write the story themselves.

A pitch letter would not usually replace an important announcement news release (see Document 5).

A pitch letter usually is offered as an exclusive to one news medium.

The key to successful pitch letters? The opening must hook the journalist. She must immediately see the story's appeal to her audience.

The Format

The pitch letter is a business letter. Use your organization's stationery, and keep the letter to one page (see the general guidelines on pp. 30–32).

The Content

First Section

The first paragraph hooks the journalist. Write it as if it were the lead of the story that you hope the reporter will write. This, of course, is an atypical beginning for a business letter, but the goal is to get the reporter to want to write the story.

Often, the first section will not mention your organization. Be concise but specific; journalists love details. Avoid the overused "Did you know . . ." opening.

This section can be one or more paragraphs.

Second Section

Tell the journalist exactly why you're writing. For example, "I think the *Dallas Morning News* should do a story on David Smith." (Smith, of course, was introduced in the first section.) If possible, praise a previous story the reporter wrote; tell him that's why you think he's the perfect writer for a story on David Smith. (Or, if the letter is addressed to an editor, mention a recent story in that editor's section, magazine, or newscast that was done well.) Give more information on David Smith. Continue to sell the story in this section.

Third Section

Note that you're offering this idea exclusively to the recipient. Then note that, because of the exclusive offer, you'll need a reply by a specific date. Next, offer help. List the best contacts from your organization and their phone numbers (be sure those contacts know). Offer to set up interviews.

Fourth Section

Tell the journalist that you'll call in a few days (name a day, if possible) to see if he is interested and to determine what help you can offer. Thank him for his time and consideration.

QUICK TIPS

- Sell the story, not your client or organization. The journalist has no interest in promoting your cause, but he does want a good story. Keep the focus on information that will appeal to the journalist's audience.
- Play fair. Reporters will never forget it if you hide bad news or if the story is old news.
- Never waste a busy journalist's time; she won't forget. The story really must be newsworthy.
- Be sure to include your direct phone number in the letter, not just a business card, which might get lost.
- Make that follow-up phone call. Do your best not to call a journalist on deadline (find out what the medium's daily deadlines are). If you can't get through to the journalist, leave a message explaining why you called. Leave no more than two messages.
- Be ready to move quickly if a reporter calls. Don't make him wait for interviews, photographs, and so on.

*Document 10, **Pitch Letter**: In this example the writer's knowledge of the recipient's staff and different newscasts presents her as a reliable partner in the creation of the proposed story. Because this letter uses the client's stationery, the writer includes her organization's name in the sign-off.*

D.W. NEWCOMER'S SONS

GENERAL OFFICES
1331 Brush Creek Boulevard   Kansas City, Missouri 64110
816/561-0024   Facsimile 816/931-7246

May 5, 1997

Mr. Tom Haldering
Assignment Editor
KCBE-TV 7
1001 Meyer
Kansas City, MO 64105

Dear Mr. Haldering:

Each year, thousands of visitors gather at Floral Hills Cemetery on Memorial Day for one of the most spectacular veterans' tributes in the country. The Avenue of Flags at Floral Hills Cemetery in Kansas City, Mo., proudly displays more than 2,760 American veterans' flags. It is the largest collection of American veterans' flags to fly on Memorial Day in the United States.

The Avenue of Flags started in 1968 with 100 flags, and now – in its 29th year – it consists of more than 2,760 flags. Together, the flags create a brilliantly colored ribbon of red, white and blue that stretches 5¼ miles.

The Avenue of Flags is open to the public throughout Memorial Day, May 26, 1997. Floral Hills Cemetery, owned and operated by D.W. Newcomer's Sons, is located at Blue Ridge and Gregory Boulevards. The cemetery opens at sunrise; all of the flags will be flying by 8 a.m.

Before dawn on Memorial Day, a 70-person crew, composed of Floral Hills employees and volunteers, begins hanging flags on the 20-foot poles. By 8 a.m., each veteran's flag is flying. This event is a good story for Lisa Morres to cover during First News. A follow-up story on what Memorial Day means to those visiting the Avenue of Flags could run during the evening newscasts.

The Avenue of Flags stems from the federal government's tradition of honoring veterans upon their death by giving an American flag to each veteran's family. Families of all American veterans are invited to donate their veterans' flags to D.W. Newcomer's Sons. The donated flags are displayed at the Avenue of Flags every Memorial Day.

We have identified a family connected with the Avenue of Flags who is willing to share their story with you and your audience. Their story is quite compelling, and I am offering it exclusively to KCBE. If you are interested, I will need to notify the family no later than Monday, May 12, 1997.

I will call you at the end of the week to determine your interest in this story. If you have any questions in the meantime, feel free to call me at 555-9127. Thank you for your time, and I look forward to working with you on the Avenue of Flags project.

Sincerely,

Amy Hunerberg
Account Executive for D.W. Newcomer's Sons
Barkley & Evergreen Public Relations

The Media Kit

The Purpose

Media kits are, in a sense, expanded news releases. They contain at least one news release (see pp. 46–56 for different types). They also contain other documents, such as backgrounders and fact sheets. Media kits can also contain photo-opportunity sheets, captioned photographs, Rolodex and business cards, product samples, and other items. The purpose of a media kit is to strengthen a journalist's interest in using your organization's news.

Media kits often are called *press kits*, a term that ignores broadcast news media. The term *media kit* can also describe a packet of information that a medium such as a magazine prepares for advertisers. That type of media kit includes advertising rate cards and reader profiles, among other items.

> The key to successful public relations media kits? They should be attractive, concise, and, if possible, include an item that will catch a busy journalist's attention. And, of course, like good news releases, they should have a local angle.

The Format

The headings of backgrounders, fact sheets, and photo-opportunity sheets are the same as those of a news release (see p. 47). That is, backgrounders, fact sheets, and photo-opportunity sheets should have a "FOR IMMEDIATE RELEASE," a composition date, a contact person (with title and phone number), and a headline or title. Each document should be labeled clearly: for example, "Backgrounder"— just as a news release is labeled "News Release."

As with news releases, put "-more-" or "-over-" at the bottom of each page except the last page, which receives a "# # #," an "end" or a "-30-." Number and slug pages starting with the second page. If a document is more than one page, use a staple, not a paper clip. Don't staple separate documents together. (Fact sheets and photo-opportunity sheets usually will be only one page.) The first page of backgrounders, fact sheets, and photo-opportunity sheets, like the first page of a news release, should be on your organization's stationery.

The Content

A media kit must contain at least one news release. The following discussion of Documents 11–13 provides additional information about media kit content.

The Backgrounder   **11**

The Purpose

The backgrounder supplements the news release. For example, a backgrounder can be a biography of a key individual mentioned in the news release. Another backgrounder could be a biography of the organization mentioned in the same news release. Like news releases, backgrounders are presented in a ready-to-publish format.

The Format

Backgrounders are double-spaced so that there is room for editing if necessary.

The headline of a backgrounder isn't like a newspaper headline—it's usually a sentence fragment. For example,

Backgrounder: Jane Smith

Remember that the heading of a backgrounder is almost the same as that for a news release, although a backgrounder is labeled as such. Review the general format guidelines under The Media Kit on p. 64.

Document 11, Backgrounder: This backgrounder supplements the news release on pp. 52–53. Like that news release, it contains no unattributed opinions.

The University of Kansas

William Allen White School of Journalism
and Mass Communications

Backgrounder

FOR IMMEDIATE RELEASE
April 15, 1996

FOR MORE INFORMATION, CONTACT:
Mike Kautsch
Professor and Dean
(913) 864-4755

The William Allen White School of Journalism and Mass Communications at the University of Kansas

In 1996, the William Allen White School of Journalism and Mass Communications at the University of Kansas is celebrating the 50th anniversary of its first graduating class.

The school grants bachelor of science and master of science degrees. Undergraduate students can specialize in advertising, business communications, magazine, newspaper or radio/television. Graduate students can specialize in newspaper/magazine, radio/television or advertising.

The school houses the editorial and advertising offices of the *University Daily Kansan*, as well as the production facilities of KJHK-FM radio and Channel 14, the school's television station. The school also produces the *Jayhawk Journalist*, a magazine for school alumni. Multimedia projects, such as a newsletter for high-school journalists that exists both on paper and as a World Wide Web site, are launched by the school's Integrated Media Lab.

The William Allen White School of Journalism and Mass Communications is located in Stauffer-Flint Hall and the Dole Human Development Center at the University of Kansas in Lawrence, Kan.

-30-

The Content

Like a news release, a backgrounder should not include unattributed opinions. Unlike a news release, a backgrounder is not meant to be an important news story. A backgrounder for a particular news release should not begin with the same who, what, when, where, why, and how opening of the news release. It generally should not have a date-line. Think of the backgrounder as a lesser, related article that will accompany the main article in the news release. A backgrounder often sounds more like an interesting encyclopedia entry than a news story.

When the backgrounder is a biography, begin by noting what the person is doing *now*. Then, perhaps in the second paragraph, return to the beginning of the person's life or career and proceed chronologically from that point.

Like a news release, a backgrounder should rarely exceed two pages.

A final caution: Don't use a backgrounder to add information that ought to be in the news release. The news release should be able to stand alone.

The Fact Sheet   12

The Purpose

The traditional fact sheet is a who, what, when, where, why, and how outline of the news release (some editors prefer this stripped-down presentation to the news release, which is potentially biased toward print media).

The Format

Fact sheets are not meant for publication in their present format. Thus, they are single-spaced, with double-spacing between paragraphs.

Remember that the heading of a fact sheet is almost the same as that of a news release, though a fact sheet, of course, is labeled as a fact sheet. Review the general format guidelines under The Media Kit on p. 64. The headline of a fact sheet often will be the good, objective headline from the news release.

The Content

A fact sheet begins with the most important area (often the *what*), then moves to the second most important area (often the *who*), and so on. As its name suggests, a fact sheet covers just the facts. There's no attempt at a story form, but it should be complete enough that a reporter could write a short news story from the fact sheet alone.

Most fact sheets arrange their text something like this:

What: The XYZ Corporation's Annual Barbecue for the United Way

Who: The XYZ Corporation is the largest employer in Central City. It makes shoelaces for . . . (You'd include more information here. You also would cover who can attend. If important or well-known people are attending, note that.)

Why: The barbecue annually raises more than $10,000 for the Central City United Way.

When: (Date and times)

Where: (Specific location, including street address, if possible)

How: (You'd cover how people can register to attend, if appropriate, and how the money is raised.)

Other fact sheets in a media kit can operate like backgrounders. They can supply background information in this "bare-bones" format. Their headlines must concisely and accurately describe the content. For example, a media kit for a basketball team might include fact sheets on player statistics, last year's record, and so forth.

Whenever possible, a fact sheet should be kept to one page.

Document 12, Fact Sheet: This fact sheet summarizes the news release on pp. 52–53. Note that the fact sheet is not as comprehensive as the news release, but it includes enough information for a reporter to write a short news story using no other sources.

The University of Kansas

William Allen White School of Journalism
and Mass Communications

Fact Sheet

FOR IMMEDIATE RELEASE
April 15, 1996

FOR MORE INFORMATION, CONTACT:
Mike Kautsch
Professor and Dean
(913) 864-4755

University of Kansas students win national journalism award

What: Students at the William Allen White School of Journalism and Mass Communications at the University of Kansas have won first place in the Print Division of the national Hearst Journalism Awards. The school receives $10,000 for its first-place finish.

The Hearst Journalism Awards often are called the Pulitzer Prizes of college journalism, said Mike Kautsch, professor and dean of the William Allen White School of Journalism and Mass Communications.

How: Students in journalism schools throughout the nation compete in the yearlong competition in such categories as in-depth writing, sports writing and opinion writing. The school that accumulates the most points throughout the year wins the competition.

Who: The William Randolph Hearst Foundation fully funds and administers the Hearst Journalism Awards.

The William Allen White School of Journalism and Mass Communications at the University of Kansas is a fully accredited school of journalism. It offers bachelor of science and master of science degrees. In 1995, the school finished second in the Hearst competition. In 1994, it finished first.

Rick Musser, Clyde M. Reed Teaching Professor of Journalism at the University of Kansas, coordinated the school's participation in the competition.

When &   The school will receive its first-place medallion and cash prize May 20, 1996,
Where: at the Hearst Journalism Awards ceremony in San Francisco.

-30-

200 Stauffer—Flint Hall · Lawrence, Kansas 66045-2350 · (913) 864-4755

13 The Photo-Opportunity Sheet

The Purpose

As their name suggests, photo-opportunity sheets are designed to attract photographers to the event you're publicizing. They are not meant for publication. Obviously, not all news releases or media kits will want or need photo-opportunity sheets. For example, a news release announcing a corporation's quarterly profits usually wouldn't have an accompanying photo-opportunity sheet—nor, ordinarily, would such a news release require a media kit.

But if your organization is sponsoring a rubber-duck race for charity—or something else that is visually interesting—a great photo opportunity exists.

The Format

Like fact sheets, photo-opportunity sheets are single-spaced, with double-spacing between paragraphs. The heading of a photo-opportunity sheet is almost the same as that for a news release, though a photo-opportunity sheet is, of course, labeled as such.

Keep the photo-opportunity sheet to one page. If you are including a large map, consider placing it on the reverse of the page.

The Content

Unlike most other media kit documents, photo-opportunity sheets can have promotional writing; your goal is to entice photographers to attend.

Be specific about times and places. Many photo-opportunity sheets include maps to advise photographers about the best shooting sites.

Document 13, Photo-Opportunity Sheet: The opening paragraphs here could be more promotional, because a photo-opportunity sheet is not meant for publication. Instead, the opening paragraphs explain why the suggested photograph would be newsworthy. The italics are optional, used only to help those paragraphs compete with the boldface items above and below.

The University of Kansas

William Allen White School of Journalism
and Mass Communications

Photo Opportunity

FOR IMMEDIATE RELEASE
April 15, 1996

FOR MORE INFORMATION, CONTACT:
Mike Kautsch
Professor and Dean
(913) 864-4755

Journalism school at University of Kansas to honor student winners of the national Hearst Journalism Awards

Students at the William Allen White School of Journalism and Mass Communications at the University of Kansas have won first place in the Print Division of the national Hearst Journalism Awards. The school receives $10,000 for its first-place finish.

The Hearst Journalism Awards often are called the Pulitzer Prizes of college journalism.

The prize-winning students will be honored in a brief ceremony Friday, April 26.

What: Awards ceremony for KU journalism students who placed in the national Hearst Journalism Awards.

Who:
- Jenni Carlson, first in sports writing.
- Colleen McCain, third in spot news and ninth in in-depth writing.
- Matt Hood, third in feature writing.
- Novelda Summers, fourth in profile writing and eighth in in-depth writing.
- Christoph Fuhrmans, fourth in sports writing and 14th in spot news.
- Virginia Margheim, seventh in profile writing.
- Rufus Coleman, 17th in opinion writing.

When: Friday, April 26, 2:30 p.m.

Where: Woodruff Auditorium, Kansas Union
University of Kansas
Lawrence, Kan.

-30-

200 Stauffer—Flint Hall · Lawrence, Kansas 66045-2350 · (913) 864-4755

A good way to organize a photo-opportunity sheet is to have

- the standard headings, as noted in the general format guidelines under The Media Kit. A photographer may have questions about lighting, shooting before or after the event, availability of key individuals, and so on. Make it easy for the photographer to contact the most knowledgeable people.
- a large, boldface "Photo-Opportunity Sheet" label
- a brief title or headline
- a short introductory, explanatory, promotional paragraph that emphasizes the visual appeal or excitement of the event
- a short review of the facts (date, time, and location); the "who, what, when . . ." format of the fact sheet works well here
- a brief discussion of what equipment and facilities are available for photographers or video crews, if any
- a map, if necessary

Writing for Broadcast Media

The Purpose

Writing for the broadcast media usually means writing for television and radio, but it can include writing for in-house corporate videos and related media.

Unfortunately, there is no "quick and (not) dirty" way to write for broadcast media. Often, knowledge of broadcast technology, music dubbing, camera angles, and much more is vital.

This section outlines three of the most common broadcast documents: broadcast news releases, radio public service announcements, and video treatments.

> The key to successful broadcast writing? Have a clear vision of what you want, and don't hesitate to seek the assistance of experienced professionals.

The Format

Use large, easily readable type.

Double-space between lines.

For more specific format guidelines for broadcast documents, see Documents 14–16.

The Content

Are you writing for television or for radio? There's a difference. Words are important in both, but more so in radio, which lacks television's immediate images.

Don't discount the possibility of images in radio, however. Evocative language and well-chosen background sounds, although not visual images, can spark an audience's imagination.

Like all forms of business communication, a broadcast production must catch and hold its audience's attention. Your production will need an opening hook. The audience must quickly discover how it will benefit by paying attention.

Initially, the possibility of being entertained will hold an audience's attention. In business communications, however, the self-interest of the audience eventually must be addressed. You must have an answer for a member of the audience who asks, "What's in this for me?"

Keep language clear and simple. Your audience can't scan back up a page for clarification.

Because the audience can't scan back up the page, don't lead with your most important point. Build up to it. Ensure that you first have the audience's attention. For that same reason, avoid beginning a sentence with an important detail.

Review "Write for the Ear, Not the Eye" in Document 24, The Speech.

Spell out large numbers. Provide phonetic spellings for unusual names or difficult words.

Use only basic punctuation marks: periods, commas, dashes, and question marks. Use ellipses (. . .) for pauses.

Avoid long, unbroken sentences. Allow the speaker(s) to breathe.

Documents 14–16 provide additional content guidelines.

14 The Broadcast News Release

The Purpose

Most radio and television stations receive news releases prepared in the standard format described in Document 5. However, it's becoming more common for such stations to receive news releases in a broadcast format.

Before writing a broadcast news release, do your research. Listen to short news items on radio and television. Study their organization, their sentence length (usually an average of 15 words), and the total time they consume (usually less than 30 seconds).

The Format

Use your organization's letterhead stationery for broadcast news releases.

The headings of a broadcast news release are, *with one exception*, those of the standard news release described in Document 5.

The one exception? Above your headline, write "Broadcast Format" in bold letters. Next to that, write the total time in seconds, of your news release. For example:

Broadcast Format—30 seconds

The Content

Begin with an interesting general statement that sets the scene for the details to come. For example: "A major employer in northwestern Oklahoma has announced new expansion plans."

Think of this general statement as a headline that attracts your audience's attention.

Whenever possible, use present tense. This differs from print news releases, which traditionally are written in past tense.

Use informal language in broadcast news releases. For example, contractions are acceptable. Strive for a casual but dignified conversational tone.

Avoid long opening phrases and clauses, and move quickly to the main point in each sentence.

Don't allow long phrases to separate subjects from their verbs.

Include people's titles before, not after, their names.

Paraphrase quotations. Don't include actual quotations unless you're including an audio cassette tape that contains the recorded quotations. (These supplied recorded quotations are called "actualities.") Quotations in broadcast news releases generally are paraphrased because listeners can't hear quotation marks, and it can be difficult to tell where a quotation begins and ends. Be sure to identify the source of a paraphrased quotation before the paraphrase.

Follow the general content guidelines provided on pp. 73–74.

15 The Radio Public Service Announcement

The Purpose

Perhaps the easiest (though not easy) broadcast document to write is a live public service announcement (PSA) for radio. Public service announcements are short messages from nonprofit, public service organizations.

If your organization is for-profit but you wish to publicize a charitable event, consider using this PSA format for a radio station's "Community Calendar" program.

The Format

The format of a PSA is straightforward:

- Produce a PSA on your organization's letterhead stationery.

QUICK TIPS

- Keep PSAs short, clear, and simple. Within those useful constraints, your message can still be dramatic.
- Many radio stations have PSA guidelines for you to follow. See what lengths (in seconds) each station prefers. Write a version of your PSA for each length; that increases the chance that the station will use one of your PSAs. If you have more than one PSA to a page, clearly separate them with white space and the ### symbol.

- If you include several PSAs to match a variety of recommended lengths:
    1. Use letterhead stationery only for the first page.
    2. Clearly label page two with a brief description and page number in the upper-right corner.
    3. Include the total time, in seconds, at the top of each individual PSA.
- At the top of the document, include the date, a contact person, that person's title, and a phone number.
- Instead of a headline, write "Public Service Announcement(s)."

Here is a sample:

Your Organization's Letterhead

August 1, 1996   For more information, contact:
                                  Jane Smith
                                  Communications Specialist
                                  (555) 111-1432

Public Service Announcement

#1–15 seconds

      Double-spaced text of PSA begins here.

The Content

Follow the general content guidelines provided on pp. 73–74.

16 The Video Treatment

The Purpose

A treatment is a pre-script document. It is an informal "short-story" version of the future video production. An experienced professional can transform your treatment into a video script.

A treatment can be part of a proposal, but more often is the first written description of a video that is scheduled for production.

The Format

Because video treatments are detailed, use short paragraphs.

Include wide margins to accommodate notes as the treatment progresses toward the script.

Single-space the treatment.

Number and label each page. Staple the pages of the treatment, or place them in a three-ring binder or folder.

The Content

Give your treatment a title.

This document is informal, but it should be detailed. Include bits of dialogue, background sounds or music, suggested camera angles—any details that will help bring your idea to life for the scriptwriter.

QUICK TIPS

- Work with the video professional as your treatment advances to script and to actual production.
- The first draft of a treatment needn't be long. Successive pre-script treatments can expand your ideas.

INTERNAL DOCUMENTS

Internal documents are the "couch potatoes" of business writing: They stay at home. They are directed to groups and individuals within your organization. Internal documents, therefore, can definitely influence your organization's success.

17 The Memorandum

The Purpose

A memorandum is a written message to an internal audience—that is, to a person or people in your organization. Think of a memo as an in-house letter. Often it is informal and conversational. The memorandum can incorporate other forms of business writing. It can be a company announcement, a modified good-news or bad-news letter, or even a policy and procedure document.

> The key to successful memos? Come to the point quickly and gracefully. Be concise.

The Format

Many organizations have memo forms that will remind you to include necessary information about:

- the date
- the recipient (a *To* section)
- the sender (a *From* section)
- the subject

At the top of the memorandum, after you record the date, record the recipient's name and title in the *To* section.

In the *From* section record your name, your title, your phone number, your office location, your department name, and, if applicable, your E-mail address. (Again, your organization's memo format may remind you of all this.)

Including all this *From* information is important. It allows the receiver to write a brief answer on your memo, cross out the original *To* and indicate that the memo should be sent back to you at the address listed in the *From* section. Or it makes it easier for her to telephone or E-mail you.

·In a memo that exists only as E-mail, be sure to include your return E-mail address. Many E-mail programs allow you to respond without entering the address.

If the memorandum is being sent to more than one person, include all the appropriate names and titles in the *To* section. You can, however, "cc" a memo if you want someone to see a memo that you've sent to someone else (see the business letter guidelines in Unit Two).

Always include a brief description of the subject in the memo's heading. (If you're writing a bad-news memo, strive for an accurate but neutral subject description.) If the memo form has no place for this, below the headings write "SUBJECT:"—and then your short description of the subject. (The subject description usually is not a complete sentence.)

A standard heading for a memo can look like this:

Date: August 1, 1996

To: Mary Jones, Director of Personnel

From: Mike Smith *MS*
Director of Communications
Ext. 3875
Building H, Office 4
Communications Dept.
msmith@xyz.com

Subject: Employee Handbook revisions

(If you're sending the memo to someone you know well, all these titles, phone numbers, and so on are probably unnecessary.)

Single-space the paragraphs of the memorandum. Double-space between paragraphs. Don't indent paragraphs.

After you have proofread the memorandum carefully, write your initials next to your name at the top of the page. This is how you sign a memo. You don't sign your name at the bottom.

The Content

Because there is no salutation at the beginning of a memo (no "Dear Ms. Jones:"), you may wish to make the first sentence particularly courteous, but don't waste time. You need to move quickly to your announced subject.

Because there's no "Sincerely" or signature at the memo's conclusion, the last words of the final paragraph should provide a sense of closure. Thanking the recipient or suggesting what the next communications action should be, or both, can provide closure.

QUICK TIPS

- Although memorandums are usually internal documents, don't write anything in a memorandum that you wouldn't want to see on the front page of the *New York Times*. Internal information has a way of becoming external. Be careful how you phrase bad news and sensitive topics. An effective test is to ask yourself, "What damage could my worst enemy or my organization's worst enemy do with this memo?" (This is good advice for writing any sensitive document, not just a memo.)
- Memorandum doesn't stand for "random memory." Its Latin ancestor is *memorare*, a verb meaning "to remember." Memorandums are relatively informal, but they still should be clear, brief, and well-organized.

In the following situations, you can use memos to advance and protect your career:

- If your organization doesn't have a standard project-status meeting or form, get in the habit of writing a memo to your boss every Friday before you leave for the weekend, one that she will receive that afternoon or Monday morning. That memo should briefly describe the status of all your projects. If you foresee problems with any of those projects, use your weekly memo to say so. If you announce a problem, also try to propose one or two solutions. If a problem does arise, you will at least have a paper trail showing your warning about it.
- Similar periodic memos can be sent to in-house clients, updating them on the progress of projects. This can be particularly useful if you have a client who is missing deadlines or whose lack of performance is affecting the quality of a project. Never threaten a client in such a memo. Diplomatically point out the financial consequences of his actions.

Document 17a, Internal Memorandum: Brevity and informality, when appropriate, are hallmarks of good internal memorandums.

GOOD FULTON & FARRELL ARCHITECTS

3102 Oak Lawn Avenue
Suite 250
Dallas, Texas 75219
214 / 528-5599
Fax 214 / 521-8672

R. Lawrence Good, FAIA
Duncan T. Fulton, FAIA
David Michael Farrell, AIA
Joseph J. Patti, AIA, CSI
Bryce A. Weigand, FAIA

Architecture
Interior Architecture
Planning

MEMORANDUM

TO: All Staff
FROM: Karen Quick, Extension 131 *KQ*
DATE: January 30, 1996

EXPENSE REPORTS ARE DUE TODAY!

Tomorrow is pay day. This pay period runs from Monday, January 15, through today = 96 hours.

As a reminder for individuals participating in the 125 Flexible Spending Accounts, this year's plan ends March 14, 1996 — only three pay periods away after tomorrow. If you have not used your allotment, now is the time to make doctor's and dentist's appointments, get your glasses or contacts, or have an artificial leg made!

F:\gff\response\mar\stafffms.jsl

*Document 17b, **External Memorandum**: External memorandums are rare, but they can be used to update clients on long-term projects.*

GOOD FULTON & FARRELL ARCHITECTS

3102 Oak Lawn Avenue	R. Lawrence Good, FAIA	Architecture
Suite 250	Duncan T. Fulton, FAIA	Interior Architecture
Dallas, Texas 75219	David Michael Farrell, AIA	Planning
214 / 528-5599	Joseph J. Patti, AIA, CSI	
Fax 214 / 521-8672	Bryce A. Weigand, FAIA	

MEMORANDUM

TO: Joe Dobbs

FROM: Duncan Fulton

DATE: February 15, 1996

RE: Sign Option Estimates

As requested in our last meeting, I have prepared conceptual cost estimates of the primary, secondary, and building sign options you selected (SK-1, SK-5 and SK-6 respectively). All sign elements were priced by two fabricators based on annotated design drawings which provided additional technical information. Please note that I have indicated the range of estimates received for these elements, while using a mid-range figure for the budget.

	Sign Type 1 Primary Sign Two-Sided	Sign Type 1 Primary Sign Single Sided	Sign Type 2 Secondary Sign	Sign Type 3 Building Sign
Sign Face Range	$2,325 - 4,298	$1,375 - 2,438	$938 - 2,025	$469 - 510
Sign Face Budget	$3,500	$2,000	$1,500	$600
Pad & Pier Foundation	1,000	1,000	---	---
Pad Only Foundation	---	---	300	---
Subtotal	$4,500	$3,000	$1,800	$600
Contingency - 15%	675	450	270	90
Cost per Unit	$5,175	$3,450	$2,070	$690
Quantity	11	11	11	6
Extended Cost	$56,925	$37,950	$22,770	$4,140

The unit costs for this work could vary greatly depending on the actual quantity of work undertaken. For the purpose of this projection, the sign fabricators were told to base their pricing on the quantity of units shown above.

The foundation pricing assumes that Sign Type 1 will be supported by a 1' x 1' x 10' grade beam with (2) - 5' piers at each end and Sign Type 2 will be supported by a 2' x 2' x 5" spread footing, without piers. If a 5' pier is desired under Sign Type 2, I estimate this will increase the per unit cost by $400 - 500.

F:\GFF\WPCORRES\FEB\CENTRE.MEM

Again, this leaves a paper trail showing that you've done your best to act in the client's interests.

If the client is someone outside your organization, a business letter may be more appropriate than a memo. However, if constant updates on an important project are advisable (as they often are), update memos are increasingly acceptable as external documents. Often, such memos are faxed or are E-mail memos.

- If an in-house client or a boss asks you to act unwisely or, worse, unethically, and you're concerned that failing to comply will get you fired, write that client or boss a memo detailing the requested action and ask if you understand correctly. If circumstances allow, consult your boss before writing to a troublesome client. Seeing the request in print may also help the client or boss perceive the unethical nature of her request. Such a memo increases the chances that the matter will be dropped—because, again, you're leaving a paper trail. A business letter can fulfill the same purpose with an external client. If the client or boss responds with a phone call, be sure to write yourself a memo (see the next paragraph).

- If you're in an unpleasant situation at work, such as giving an employee a poor evaluation or firing an employee, write a memo to yourself, simply for your own files, describing what happened. Be brief but accurate and detailed. Be certain to date the memo. That memo can help refresh your memory later if you need to describe the situation to internal or even external authorities.

The Company Announcement 18

The Purpose

The goal of a company announcement is to disseminate the facts to all appropriate employees as quickly as possible. The reason is simple: The employees of your organization shouldn't hear the news elsewhere first.

The company announcement is difficult to define because it can address so many subjects—stock news, cafeteria menus, obituaries—and can be conveyed by so many media (for example, old-fashioned bulletin-board announcements, memos, memos read at meetings, E-mail, and the like). Of these media, bulletin-board announcements, memos, and E-mail are perhaps used most.

> The key to successful company announcements? Speed, brevity, and diplomacy.

The Format

Most company announcements are single-spaced and dated. For example, a date at the bottom of a bulletin-board announcement shows both the timeliness of the announcement and where it ends; it can be the equivalent of a "-30-" (see the general guidelines for the news release).

Most company announcements are short. Try to keep E-mail announcements to 10 lines or fewer so that they'll fit onto the screen.

To save space in company announcements, E-mail or not, you may want to indent paragraphs rather than double-spacing between them.

The Content

The following examples show types of information that can be communicated using company announcements.

Announcements That Affect Stock Prices

If the announcement affects your organization's stock, timing is crucial. The announcement often is made when the stock markets are closed—and it is made simultaneously to the news media, major stockholders, and the employees. If the announcement were made to the employees first and they were able to sell or buy their organization's stock with that insider knowledge, both you and they would have broken the law. Keep all such announcements strictly confidential until the moment of release. Never use your insider knowledge to

QUICK TIPS

- Speculation (Avoid It)
  In all company announcements, state nothing but the facts (and sometimes, as in obituaries, don't state all the facts). Never speculate. The only place for anything speculative is in an approved quotation.

- Employee Titles
  In the first reference to an employee in a company announcement, include that employee's title (this doesn't apply to the headline). The *Associated Press Stylebook* recommends capitalizing a title when it comes immediately before a name and lowercasing titles in all other instances. However, many employees won't understand that; thus it can be best to capitalize all employee titles in all instances.

- Employees' Families
  Remember that many employees have families that can be affected by an important announcement. When appropriate and possible, include your awareness of that fact in the announcement. Cover what the announcement means to families. (This is a good policy for all internal documents.)

- Editing the Announcement
  Get "fingerprints" on the announcement. Have it reviewed both by your boss and by legal counsel, if possible and appropriate.

- Distribution
  If the distribution of the announcement is complex, have a written timetable that specifies how each step of the distribution will be handled—that is, when each step will happen, how it will happen, and who is in charge of that step. This helps motivate employees to be certain that they flawlessly perform their portions of the task.

  Take particular care to ensure distribution to high-ranking officials in your organization. They no doubt know about the announcement, but they'll want to see that the announcing mechanism works.

Document 18, Company Announcement: JCPenney places company announcements on controlled-access bulletin boards throughout its headquarters. Updated daily, the bulletin boards function as a daily newsletter.

DECA honors JCPenney for 50 years of support

Two young leaders from Distributive Education Clubs of America (DECA) recently presented Vice Chairman Jim Oesterreicher with an award certain to have made James Cash Penney proud. On Feb. 27, DECA National President Geoff Basye and Vice President Torenon Busby honored JCPenney with a marble plaque for its support in preparing high school students for careers in the marketing industry — an effort that began with Mr. Penney a half century ago.

Mr. Penney was a founding member of DECA, which was established in 1946. He and leaders of other corporations formed the organization to promote marketing education for young people.

DECA encourages students to enter into the marketing and retail fields through work-study programs at high schools across the nation. Students spend part of the day in class and the other part working as interns at local businesses or organizations. Members of DECA also have the opportunity to participate in local, regional, and national competitions that use integral learning activities to evaluate a student's knowledge and skills in marketing and management occupations.

"You can sit in a classroom for two hours and read about retail and marketing," Basye says. "But the hands-on experience you get from working in the field and talking to people who deal with those issues every day is equally important."

Each year, JCPenney sponsors a DECA scholarship program that provides $1,000 grants to 20 high school seniors based on their academic and personal achievements. Students who enter must plan on attending a two-year or four-year program to major in marketing management or marketing education. JCPenney also supports DECA's Retail Merchandising competitions.

DECA President Geoff Basye, JCPenney Vice Chairman Jim Oesterreicher, and DECA Vice President Torenon Busby

3/1-5/96

purchase or sell stock. Whenever possible, work with your organization's legal counsel on such announcements.

Obituaries

The headline of the announcement usually is just the employee's name. It is best not to list the cause of death. That omission can start rumors, but it also avoids occasionally awkward situations. Don't be afraid to use the word "died"; it's better than "passed away" or other euphemisms.

An objective tone is best. Leave the sentiment to a manager's quotation. (You won't sound heartless; the organization's grief will appear in that quotation.) Note the former employee's age. Outline the employee's career with the organization. List survivors. With the family's permission, include information on memorials and/or funeral arrangements (this sometimes can be a veiled reference to the cause of death: "The family requests that any memorial donations be made to the Cancer Program at City Hospital."). Do not include information about who will replace the deceased employee. That's a topic for another company announcement.

New Employee/Retiring Employee

When a new employee is scheduled to join your organization, use a company announcement to tell employees something about him. For example, what is the new hire's educational background and work experience?

Similarly, when an employee retires, announce that and trace her career with the company. Consider including a quotation from a co-worker that praises the departing employee.

The Policy and Procedure Document 19

The Purpose

Policy and procedure documents take many forms: binders, magazines, memos, brochures, and so on. All share a common goal: to communicate clearly how something works or how something should be done. In short, policy and procedure documents are explanations.

The key to successful policy and procedure documents? Consistent sentence structure, logical organization, and clarity.

The Format

Select a layout that aids comprehension. Consider using:

- bullets (•)
- internal headlines
- descriptors (short summaries placed in the margins next to the passage they describe)
- illustrations or photographs
- white space (so that the document doesn't look cluttered and overwhelming)

The Content

Consistent Sentence Structure

Within the document, always address the same audience. Don't switch back and forth from "You should" to "The employee should."

Select either the indicative or imperative (command) mood, and, as much as possible, stick with your choice.

Indicative mood: The employee should sign the voucher.
Imperative mood: Sign the voucher.

Use active voice as much as possible (some situations may require passive voice).

Active voice: Sign the voucher.
                 The employee should sign the voucher.
Passive voice: The voucher should be signed by the employee.

Document 19, Policy and Procedure Document: Brevity, short paragraphs, and the generous use of white space make this a reader-friendly document.

Policy: ADM01003
Date: 03/21/96 (new)
        mm/dd/yy (rev)

ARIZONA STATE RETIREMENT SYSTEM

POLICIES & PROCEDURES

FILE SYSTEM

Policies and Procedures for ASRS File System

Purpose: To establish guidelines for filing ASRS documents

Authority: The Support Team

Policy: The ASRS shall maintain a Central File System

Procedure: 1) The Support Team is responsible for effectively filing all documents from the Director's Office.

2) Members of the Support Team are required to do their filing either in the morning or in the evening before they leave.

3) Each member of the Support Team is required to use the filing system now in place.

4) If other individuals [e.g., A.D.'s, other staff] need a file, document, report, etc., they are required to fill out a request slip identifying the requested document(s) and expected length of time the document(s) will be used.

5) A member of the Support Team is responsible for retrieving and returning the item(s).

Logical Organization

Establish a logical order for the process you're explaining. For example, chronological, most important to least important, or clustering of related points.

Keep policy and procedure documents short and logical. In unavoidably long documents, look for logical ways to cluster the information into brief, well-labeled sections.

Clarity

Avoid "bizspeak"—that is, inflated and pretentious words. Use clear English.

Tighten flabby sentences. Come to the point, but do avoid being so abrupt that you sound rude.

Avoid long paragraphs.

20 The Business Report

The Purpose

Business reports communicate facts and, sometimes, opinions or recommendations based on those facts.

> The key to successful business reports? Whether formal or informal, all good business reports are clear, concise, and well-organized.

The Format

The format of a business report should assist organization and aid readability. That can mean using:

- large type on the cover (larger than ordinary text type)

- internal headlines or section titles (boldface and/or larger than ordinary text type)
- margins of at least one inch
- white space between sections
- charts and graphs, when appropriate, to reinforce and clarify meaning

The text of a report is single-spaced. Double-space between paragraphs, and don't indent them. Finally, number the pages of the report.

The Content

Getting Started

Before beginning the report, ask yourself these questions:

- What is the purpose of the report? Does everyone involved agree?
- Who is the audience? What does it expect, want, and need to learn from this report?

Let the answers to those questions shape all the information the report contains.

A formal business report contains the following sections. (Less formal versions can discard some of these.)

Letter or Memo of Transmittal

This is typically paper-clipped to the report. Such a document essentially says, "Attached is the report you requested. If you have questions, please contact me." (This is a matter of courtesy—always an important part of effective business communications.)

Title Page

This includes a title, a descriptive subtitle if necessary, the name(s) of the author(s), and the date. The title page should clearly communicate that the document is a report on a specific topic.

Table of Contents

A table of contents lists the starting page for each section, not the span of pages for each section. Don't include the letter or memo of transmittal or the title page here.

Table of Charts and Graphs

If you decide to include this, the standard title is "Table of Charts and Graphs."

Executive Summary

An executive summary is a concise, one-page (if possible) overview of the report's highlights. This is needed only if the report is formal and long—but it is often a good idea to include one. Bullets (•) can be useful here.

Text of the Report

The text generally consists of an introduction, a body, and a conclusion. Announce the report's purpose and main point(s), explain and develop the purpose and main point(s), and, in closing, reassert the purpose and main point(s). This applies whether the report is two pages or 200.

Introduction

The introduction states the report's purpose and main point(s). The introduction also establishes the tone of the report and the level of the language used.

If your introduction seems too brief, consider two things:

- Brevity in a report is an asset as long as it's not confusing or rude.
- If the introduction seems so brief that it's ungraceful, beef it up by announcing the organization of the report. That is, use the introduction to forecast the order of the sections to come. This may repeat some of the table of contents, but such repetition can reinforce the report's organization.

Don't let the executive summary steal the function of the introduction. The introduction should be written as if the executive summary didn't exist.

Body

The body delivers the specifics. It explains and develops the main point(s). In most reports, the introduction and conclusion are short; the body is comparatively long.

In a short report, the "subject, restriction, information" paragraph-organization technique can help keep the body in line with the subject of the report. In other words, each time a new section of the body begins, the opening sentence refers to the subject of the report and to the restriction of the subject covered in the new section. Specific information follows. For example, here is a subject-restriction transitional sentence: "A second reason we should close the Arcadia factory [subject] is that its equipment is obsolete [restriction]." The information following this sentence would prove that the equipment is, indeed, obsolete.

The sections of the body should be organized logically—for example, from the first event in time to the last, from the most important information to the least, from the best solution to the worst, and so forth. Consider using internal headlines to mark off sections or chapters in the body.

If the report makes recommendations, develop them in the body. You may wish to announce them in the introduction. In the body, you can either put the evidence first, so that when you make the recommendations, they seem logical—or, if there are several recommendations, you may wish to make them one at a time and, after each, provide evidence to support it.

Conclusion

The conclusion reasserts the purpose and main point(s) in light of all the information in the body.

The conclusion can also note the next action that will or should be taken.

If the conclusion seems too short, it can briefly note the most useful sources of information. (Remember: Unless brevity seems rude or graceless, it is an asset, not a problem.)

Endnotes (Often Called Footnotes)

Endnotes cite specific sources of information. They're needed only in very formal reports.

List of Works Consulted

Like endnotes, a list of resources is reserved for very formal reports.

Appendix

An appendix would contain supporting articles, tables, charts, and other related information. An appendix is optional.

INTERNAL/EXTERNAL DOCUMENTS

Internal/external documents are like well-behaved children: They're great at home, but you can also send them out into the world. For example, your organization may have one newsletter for employees and another for clients. You may write one speech to be delivered to employees and another to be delivered at a professional organization's annual convention.

21 The Newsletter/Magazine Story

The Purpose

A newsletter/magazine story delivers many facts on an important topic to a large, well-defined audience. Such stories usually can be read in one sitting and are designed either to inform or to entertain as well as inform.

The key to successful newsletter/magazine stories? Show readers immediately why they'll benefit from reading the story. Show them that they'll learn important information and that they may even be entertained as they learn.

Most newsletter and magazine stories fall into one of three categories:

1. straight news stories
2. features (often called "narratives")
3. hybrids

The content of each of these three is discussed following the format guidelines below.

The Format

Double-space the text, and indent the paragraphs.

On page one, include a headline, a subhead (if necessary), and a byline. If your story is done on a computer networked with other computers, you may also wish to record the file name so that story editors can display your story on their screens.

Put "-more-" at the bottom of each appropriate page.

Beginning with page two, in the upper-right corner, place a slug (a brief description of the story), a page number, and your last name. For example: "Bubblegum-2 Smith."

Put "-30-," or "# # #," or "endit" at the story's conclusion.

Quick Tips

- Be guided by a clear understanding of audience and purpose. Know who your audience is and what its interests in this situation are. Be able to define, for yourself, the story's purpose in one clear sentence.
- Do rigorous research. Gather *more* information than will ultimately appear in the story. The extra information will help you see what should be in the story. It also gives you more options as you write, and it can save you from embarrassing mistakes.
- Read other newsletters and magazines. Analyze what works and what doesn't.
- Use specifics, not generalities. Don't *say* that a person is busy. *Show* that she is busy.

The Content

Straight News Stories

Straight news stories begin with a lead (an opening paragraph or paragraphs) that incorporates the most important details of who, what, when, where, why, and, sometimes, how. Information is written in descending order of importance. (Leads don't have to include every detail of who, what, when, where, why, and how—just those areas that are key to easily understanding the story. Why and how, for example, may not be that crucial and can be covered later in the story.)

The straight news story is, except for the format, nearly identical to the "announcement" form of the news release (see Document 5). In a straight news story, the focus is on informing readers, not on entertaining them.

Features/Narratives

Similar to straight news stories, features (or narratives) inform, but they also entertain. Storytelling skills are important in features. For

National File Clean-Up Planned To Promote Recycling

A first national "Clean Your Files Day" is planned for April, in time for Earth Day celebrations on April 22. The spring cleaning will collect thousands of tons of unneeded office paper for recycling. Leading the file purge charge will be office workers and city employees in communities throughout the U.S.– San Diego, Des Moines, Louisville, Austin, and others.

"We're participating in 'Clean Your Files Day' because we recognize it as a tremendous opportunity to promote our recycling programs and educate our 12,000 city employees," said William Rhodes, solid waste services director for the city of Austin.

"Clean Your Files Day" was first launched last year in Chicago, where participating employees recovered up to twelve times their normal rate of waste paper for recycling. In one building alone, 3,500 employees recovered 27 tons of office paper in just one day.

For more information, including a free "Clean Your Files Day" guidebook, fun fact sheets, and camera-ready logos, contact the National Office Paper Recycling Project at (202) 223-3088; fax, (202) 429-0422. ■

Document 21a, Straight News Story: In this story, the lead includes where, what, when, why, and who. Information becomes progressively less important as the story nears its conclusion.

Source: *Nation's Cities Weekly* 19(14): 4 (April 8, 1996). Reprinted by permission.

example, the lead—unlike the lead of a straight news story—need not present all the most important facts. Instead, it should "hook" the reader. That is, it should make the reader want to read the story.

Details can be presented creatively in a feature. For example, a writer was once assigned a story on the sale of a retailer's one-million-lionth pair of pantyhose. Instead of writing a straight news story, he calculated that a kicking chorus line of one million pantyhose wearers would stretch from New York City to Little Rock, Arkansas. He then determined how far into outer space the unraveled thread from one million pairs of pantyhose would reach. It was a popular, entertaining, memorable story.

In a straight news story, the conclusion is the least important section. In a feature, however, the conclusion may be the most important section. At worst, it's second only to the lead in dramatic value.

Rhetorical strategies listed in "Rhetoric and Business Writing" (see Unit One) can work well in a feature.

Lead strategies

Various hook-lead strategies can strengthen your feature:

- a snappy, one-sentence teaser that creates a mystery. Example: "Night after night, it troubled him." (What troubled him? Who is he? What was going on night after night? Why did it go on night after night? Why did it happen at night?) The reader will continue, wanting to solve the mysteries.
- a short, interesting anecdote that illustrates the story's main point
- an interesting comment from someone involved in the story
- an impressive fact (be sure it's truly impressive and interesting)
- a striking image
- a thought-provoking question that can't be answered with a simple yes or no

In other words, in most features the lead isn't as direct as that of a straight news story. Since a feature lead doesn't have to announce what the story is about, it can develop a tightly focused hook that compels the reader to keep reading.

Feature organizational schemes

There are many ways to organize a feature. One element most of the schemes share, however, is a "nut graf," or "nut paragraph." A nut graf isn't the story's first paragraph, but it does come early in the story. It puts the lead into the broader context of the story. It announces the story's topic. It's also called a "swing graf" because it swings the lead into the true focus of the story. One rule of thumb is to get the nut graf as close to the beginning of the story as possible. Don't keep the hooked reader wondering about the exact topic of the story.

Here are six good organizational schemes for features:

The *Wall Street Journal* Style #1

Many *WSJ* features begin with a tightly focused anecdote. Then comes the nut graf. More anecdotes then lead to more information—or more information is followed by illustrative anecdotes—or both. The feature often closes with an anecdote that either sums up the story or adds a

Document 21b, Feature: This story strives to entertain as it informs. The story uses the "theme" organizational scheme (see p. 106), incorporating as many humorous football and landscaping references as possible.

Nobody—but *nobody*—kicks KU's grass

INJURIES AND PENALTIES ARE NOTHING NEW TO FOOTBALL, BUT SEVERAL KU STUDENTS were caught off guard, so to speak, when campus police cited them for unnecessary roughness to grass. On the defensive are eight KU students who scrimmaged last December on the rain-soaked lawn in front of Fraser Hall. Fifteen yards and a loss of down apparently won't suffice: The undergraduate sodbusters will tackle the local legal system this month, and the misdemeanor charge of tearing up the turf carries the possibility of both a fine and a jail sentence.

An official of the Lawrence Municipal Court recently told reporters from the University Daily Kansan that although the KU Eight had walked all over the rights of the grass, he doubted that they faced a stint in jail. If found guilty, the students may have to pay their debt to society through a specified amount of community-service work.

Meanwhile, the alleged victim has made no comment, and a grassroots support movement for the defendants continues to grow.

Source: *Kansas Alumni* (March 1985). Reprinted by permission.

twist to the main point. Occasionally, it closes with a quotation, from someone involved, that seems to sum up the main point.

The *Wall Street Journal* Style #2

Many *WSJ* features begin with a snappy, one-sentence lead; that one sentence gets its own paragraph. The sentence doesn't explain the story. Instead, it's usually a little mysterious. Readers, therefore, read the story to solve the mystery of the lead.

Immediately after that snappy sentence comes the nut graf, which announces the focus of the story.

From this point on, the organization is similar to the organization that follows the nut graf in style #1, described above.

The difference between these two *Wall Street Journal* styles is the lead's length and snappiness. The features in the *Wall Street Journal* can provide excellent instruction in feature writing.

The *People* Magazine Personality Profile

Many such profiles begin with an anecdote that tantalizes readers. The goal of the anecdote is to make readers ask, "How in the world did the person get into this situation? What's the story behind this? And what will be the result?" This opening anecdote often is a key dramatic point in the person's life. Frequently, it's a turning point.

Next comes the nut graf, an explanation of the anecdote, in which those questions may be partially answered.

Next comes the history of the central figure. The history helps explain the opening anecdote. It often includes comments from the central figure. The history continues until the story reaches, or begins to reach, the resolution of that opening anecdote.

The conclusion returns to the present and shows readers what the central figure is doing now. If the opening anecdote hasn't been resolved, the final resolution is presented here. The feature often closes with a pithy quotation from the central figure.

The Epic Poetry Scheme

People magazine personality profiles are based on the epic poetry scheme (remember *The Iliad* and *The Odyssey*?). Epic poetry begins *in medias res*—that is, "in the middle of things," usually at an exciting moment. This leads readers to ask two questions: "How did we get here?" and "What will happen next?"

The epic poem then flashes back to the beginning, takes us to the middle (which we already know), skips that, and moves to a dramatic conclusion.

The Bookend Scheme

The story begins with a strong, appropriate, compelling image that captures the reader's interest. The story later closes with the same image—but with a twist. The image operates as a set of bookends—one bookend at the beginning of the story and one, with a twist, at the end.

The Theme Scheme

This is very similar to the bookend scheme, but instead of just appearing twice, the image is woven throughout the story. For example, if you were to compare someone's life to that of a fairy-tale princess (which probably would be a little trite), a unifying element throughout the story might be references to fairy-tale images: handsome princes, giants, witches, fairy godmothers, and so on. Such a technique is also called an extended metaphor. It works best with short features.

Document 21c, Hybrid: This magazine story's first sentence contains entertaining, conversational opinions ("yet another" and "stunning") to attract reader attention. A more pronounced straight-news tone begins with the second paragraph and continues to the conclusion.

NEWS ANALYSIS

New player emerges on trade side

BY LORNE MANLY

The publishing industry is welcoming yet another financial player to its ranks after the stunning denouement culminating in the sale of 13 Reed Elsevier PLC medical titles to New York City-based investment firm M.E. Zukerman & Co.

PressCorps Inc.—backed by merchant bankers Ladenburg, Thalmann & Co. and other investors—thought it was on the verge of a deal for the Excerpta Medica titles. But Reed Elsevier jilted the suitors and instead chose Zukerman & Co. Sources say the price tag is between $18.5 million and $19 million. Stephen Stoneburn, most recently the president of Argus Integrated Media, will serve as president and CEO of the yet-to-be-renamed company.

The purchase represents Zukerman & Co.'s first foray into the business-to-business publishing arena. The eight-year-old firm currently has holdings in manufactur-

ing, energy and consumer-product companies. Principal David Straden says Zukerman & Co. was attracted by trade publishing's stability and growth potential. The company's near-term focus is to build on its base of medical titles, but there are plans to expand into other areas—most likely the industrial, financial services and legal fields.

The goal: $100 million in revenues in three to four years. The firm has made 10 transactions in the past three years and is a relatively long-term investor, usually waiting five to seven years before seeking an exit.

PressCorps, meanwhile, is moving ahead with a project that would have tied into the Excerpta deal. The New York City-based company is in talks with investment bankers about funding a new consumer title called *Healing* that would target college-educated women in their thirties and address issues of physical, spiritual and mental health. □

Source: *Folio:* 25(7): 496 (May 1, 1996). Reprinted by permission.

The conclusion

Many features return to a tight focus in the conclusion. One good conclusion strategy is to return to the image, question, or anecdote developed in the lead, and put a new but appropriate twist on it. The lead thus is seen in a new light or is better understood. Sometimes the conclusion can provide the end of an anecdote that began in the lead.

Remember: The most important fact can appear in the feature's conclusion. In that case, the rest of the story must be so good that the reader will keep reading until she learns that fact.

Hybrids

The hybrid is a compromise between the straight news story and the feature. To hook the reader, it begins with a feature-like lead. Then, to save space, it uses a nut graf that swings the story into a straight news approach. Hybrids lack the strong, dramatic conclusions that characterize features. The hybrid can be a good short form for newsletters.

The Proposal 22

The Purpose

A proposal is a document that describes and promotes an idea—for a new magazine, a new departmental structure, an expensive media kit, and so forth. In addition to describing the idea, it describes a way to realize the idea.

The key to successful proposals? Clear organization and specifics that show how the idea solves a well-defined problem or seizes a well-defined opportunity.

The Format

The format of a proposal should assist organization and aid readability. That can mean using:

- large type on the cover (larger than ordinary text type)
- internal headlines or section titles (boldface and/or larger than ordinary text type)
- margins of at least one inch
- white space between sections. (Consider beginning each new section on a new page with a clear section title.)
- charts and graphs, when appropriate, to reinforce and clarify meaning

The text of a proposal is single-spaced. Double-space between paragraphs, and don't indent them. Number the pages of the proposal—usually starting not with the table of contents but with the executive summary, if that section follows the table of contents.

The Content

Letter or Memo of Transmittal

Attach a brief cover letter or memo addressed to your audience, essentially saying, "Here is a proposal for you." It can close with an implicit or explicit request for action, such as "I'm available to discuss this at your convenience." A "Thank you for your time and consideration" can follow the request.

The Proposal

The proposal itself should be tailored to the situation—but in general, it should include the following sections (you needn't use these particular titles for each section). The order of presentation here reflects the order in a traditional proposal.

Title page

Your title should be attractive, positive, and descriptive. Often, a snappy title with a descriptive, positive subtitle is effective. The descriptive subtitle should make it clear that the document is a proposal. For example:

GIVE ALL YOU CAN

A Blood Drive Proposal for XYZ Corporation

You also may wish to include a "Presented by Your Name." Many title pages include the date at the bottom.

Table of contents

(Don't include the letter or memo of transmittal or the title page in the table of contents.) A table of contents lists just the starting page for each section, not the span of pages for each section.

Executive summary

This is brief (a page or less, if possible). It lists the highlights of the proposal. It's a quick summary for a busy executive. It should be written as if the rest of the proposal didn't exist and vice versa: The proposal should be written as if the *executive summary* didn't exist. In this way, the proposal itself will introduce each point as if for the first time. The proposal won't rely on the executive summary for such introductions.

Situation analysis (the problem or opportunity)

This section is a description of the status quo. It should make clear the need for—or the advantages of—change. The situation analysis should create a sense of need or desire. Don't mention the program or project that you're proposing. Describe only the situation to be affected by that program or project. Do not mention that action is desirable or forthcoming. (The only exception to this is when the program or project is part of the situation. For example, if you're writing a proposal for the latest version of an annual blood drive, it's all right to mention that a program or project is needed.)

The plan (goals, objectives, recommended actions)

- Begin by announcing the proposal's *purpose:* to present a plan that will improve the status quo. Include a short overview of your plan, but leave the specifics for the goals, objectives, and recommended actions.

  After announcing the proposal's purpose but before moving to the specific goals, objectives, and recommended actions, you may wish to include a short section describing the audiences that the proposal targets.

- The plan often begins with a *goal*, which is a strong, clear, succinct statement of intent. A goal is an announcement of your intent to affect the situation described in the previous section.

  Most goals begin with a strong infinitive: "To increase corporate blood donations . . ." When possible, goals are measurable: "To increase corporate blood donations by 20 percent . . ."

  When appropriate, goals include a deadline as well:

  GOAL: To increase corporate blood donations by 20 percent by March 1.

  A plan can have more than one goal. For example, a second goal for an employee blood drive might be to increase employee morale or the organization's visibility in the community.

- *Objectives* are the steps to be met to realize your goal fully. Thus, a goal is a broad, encompassing statement. Objectives are narrower, aimed at specific achievements that must occur if the goal is to be reached. Like a goal, most objectives begin with a strong infinitive. Each objective ideally addresses a single, specific area. When appropriate, they include a measurement of success and a deadline:

  OBJECTIVE #1: To publicize the blood drive to all employees by February 25.

  OBJECTIVE #2: To publicize the blood drive to all city residents by February 25.

  One approach to determining what your objectives should be is to have at least one objective for each targeted audience. A targeted audience could receive more than one objective.

- *Recommended actions* are the steps that must be taken to reach each objective. Recommended actions usually begin with commands: "Write, mail, telephone," and so on. Each action details a single, specific step. Each objective is followed immediately by its recommended actions.

  Under each recommended action, you may wish to elaborate upon the action and include matters such as cost and deadlines. If so, watch your verb tense. Be consistent. Don't switch back and forth between *is*, *will*, and *would*.

  GOAL: To increase corporate blood donations by 20 percent by March 1.

  OBJECTIVE #1: To publicize the blood drive to all employees by February 25.

RECOMMENDED ACTIONS:

1. Create E-mail message by February 1.
   (Description of message goes here.)
   (Cost goes here.)
2. Place E-mail message by February 15.

OBJECTIVE #2: To publicize the blood drive to all city residents by February 25.

RECOMMENDED ACTIONS:

1. Prepare news release for city media
   (Description of release goes here.)
   (Cost goes here.)

Ideally, the goals, objectives, and recommended actions section should leave the reader with few or no questions about the details. That is, sizes, colors, and content should be specified as much as possible, especially in the recommended actions. If this becomes too detailed and is bogging down the section, you can include details in the Supplements section and simply tell the reader to consult that section.

Timetable

This information often is included automatically in the goals, objectives, and recommended actions. In other words, this section is optional. As a separate section, however, it can be a useful chart, with the date to the left and a description of what happens on that date to the right. For example:

February 1   Post bulletin-board posters.
February 15 Place message in electronic mail.

Budget

Again, this may already be covered under recommended actions, but it also should be a separate section. List the sources of your information; use the line-item approach with a total at the bottom. For example:

Posters, 40 copies (Acme Printing) $100.00
Buttons, 100 items (ABC Button Co.) . . $ 50.00
TOTAL. $150.00

In a very detailed budget, it can be a good idea to include a "contingency budget" for unforeseen expenses. The standard way to do this is to total all other expenses and list that amount as a subtotal. Next determine what 10 percent of that subtotal is and list the 10 percent as your contingency budget. Then add the subtotal and the contingency budget for your total. (Do your best not to spend that contingency money.)

Challenges

This section presents and refutes challenges to the proposed actions. It is optional, though desirable when obvious objections exist. Usually, the challenge is clearly issued and then is refuted. For example:

CHALLENGE: Employees don't read the bulletin boards, so they will not see the posters.

REFUTATION: Because the posters will be bright green, they will stand out from XYZ Corporation's usual black and white posters. The unusual color will attract the attention of passing employees.

Additional benefits

This optional section details the "add-on" benefits that your proposal would generate besides the basic benefit of reaching the established goal(s). For example, your blood drive might help recruit good new community-minded job applicants. You can simply list these as ADDITIONAL BENEFIT #1, and so on.

Evaluation

Note how you plan to evaluate the success of your proposal. What systems of measurement will you use? Measurable goals and objectives will make evaluation easier.

QUICK TIP

- Be diplomatic. Don't present your proposal as the savior of a sinking ship. Your proposal often will target an area managed by the very people who will evaluate your idea. Don't hurt their feelings or make them defensive. Such diplomacy is particularly important in the situation analysis.

Conclusion

This is brief. Be certain to reassert specifically what you've proposed. Mention again the theme or slogan or product. This section can include an implicit or explicit recommendation for action.

Supplements

This section can include samples, dummy layouts, charts, graphs, and articles—any material that the proposal calls for (and any material that supports the clarity and integrity of the proposal). Nothing should be in the Supplements section that isn't referred to earlier in the proposal.

The Brochure 23

The Purpose

A brochure usually is a promotional booklet or pamphlet that contains information about your product, service, or organization.

The key to successful brochures? Eye-catching design, logical organization, and specific details.

The Format

The old architectural maxim applies here: Form follows function. How will the brochure be used? Mailed in a standard business envelope? Posted with thumbtacks on a bulletin board? Accessed through Internet? Filed away for future reference? Its intended use can determine format. The most common brochure format is an 11" x 8½" sheet of paper with three equal panels on each side (a six-panel brochure). It fits conveniently into business envelopes and files and, with good design, also can function as a bulletin-board poster.

When you are designing a brochure, use internal headlines to label sections. Those headlines can help you maintain readers' interest.

The Content

As always, content is determined by the audience you're addressing and the message you want to send. Be sure that you know both areas well.

Remember the KISS acronym: *Keep It Short and Simple*. Study other successful brochures. Note how concise they are.

Organization of information depends on your topic and the audience you're addressing. Usually a brochure is designed to begin with general information and move to more specific information. Different sections are short and clearly labeled. Information mentioned in a general introduction can be explored in greater depth later in the brochure.

Another useful acronym is AIDA: *Attention, Interest, Desire, and Action*.

- Begin by effectively grabbing your readers' Attention. Immediately focus upon *their* self-interest.
- Now that you have their Attention, hold their Interest by keeping the focus on their wants and needs.
- As you keep their Interest, build Desire within them. That Desire is related to your brochure's goal—to have people buy the product, apply for employment at your organization, sign up for a particular service, and so forth.
- Now that your readers are eager, give them the information they need to take Action. That may be a phone number, an application form, or a date/time/place.

Graphics (photos, illustrations, easy-to-read charts) can help you win Attention and keep Interest.

If you've built a message that satisfies both KISS and AIDA, test it using the standard five W's and an H. Have you covered the important parts of who, what, when, where, why, and how? Have you done so in a logical order?

Quick Tips

- Good design is important in every document, but it's particularly important in a brochure. The design should attract readers and enhance readability.
- In most documents, the words are written first and the document is designed around them. In a brochure, you may wish to select the most functional format and make your words fit that. (A similar notion applies in business letters, which are limited by traditional format to one page.)
- Should your brochure be interactive? Should it contain a toll-free 800 number? A fax-on-demand phone number? An E-mail or web address? A street or post-office-box address? All of the above? Consider two-way communication tactics as you prepare your brochure.

The Speech 24

The Purpose

A business speech is a performance—a scripted monologue performed in front of an audience. It contains a main point, and it explains and elaborates upon that main point.

The key to successful speeches? Keep them short, well-organized, and aimed at the audience's self-interest.

The Format

Triple- or quadruple-space between the lines of each draft for the speaker. Use large type and wide margins.

Type only on the upper two-thirds of each page so that the speaker's chin doesn't dip too low to her chest as she reads.

Number the pages. Put "-more-" at the bottom of each appropriate page. Put "-end-" at the end of the speech.

Don't staple the speech—the pages must turn easily. See what the speaker is comfortable with. Some speakers prefer that the speech be three-hole punched and placed in a notebook.

Spell out big numbers for the speaker. Consider phonetically spelling tough words or tough names for the speaker. See what she is comfortable with.

If you use visual supplements, note in the text of the speech where they go so that the speaker can pause and, perhaps, gesture at the screen.

Include "stage directions" in the speech in parentheses. For example, suggest a dramatic pause at a particular point by writing "PAUSE HERE" in the text of the speech. You can also suggest gestures.

The Content

Begin by Evaluating Five Things:

1. *The purpose*. After discussing this with the speaker, write, in one sentence, the main point of the speech. Then write a brief synopsis. Create a working title. Have the speaker review this and get his input.

2. *The listeners (the audience)*. Who are they? What is their common background? What is their strong self-interest in this situation? What topics can the speaker discuss that are sure to draw a response? What are their expectations? You'll keep them interested if they're hearing about themselves. (Remember: They hope to be informed and entertained.)

3. *The speaker*. Be sure to write *his* speech—not yours. The speech should sound like the speaker at his best—not you at yours. Spend as much time as possible with the speaker to learn any favorite phrases, gestures, and the like.

4. *The time frame*. Has a set time been allocated for the speech? If not, consider the subject, purpose, audience, and speaker in determining how long the speech should be. Whenever possible, limit the speech to 20 minutes or less.

5. *The setting*. Where will the speech be given? Will the location be outside or inside? What is the size of the room? Will there be a lectern and microphone? Will audio-visual equipment be available if needed? Will a glass and a pitcher of water be provided?

Organize the Speech Logically and Gracefully

There are many ways to organize a speech. Virtually all speeches have an introduction, a body, and a conclusion. Most business speeches have a "what" and a "why," announcing and explaining a main point. These two elements are the foundations of the following two organizational schemes.

Organizational scheme #1

Use this scheme when the "what" is more important than the "why." Use it when you want the audience to be able to repeat the main point to others.

- *Introduction*: Build up to the "what" (the main point) and announce it. If the "what" is something positive that you want to emphasize, make it the last words of the introduction and pause after it.

- *Body*: Expand on the "what." One of the best ways to flesh out the main point is to explain what it means to the audience.

    Another good way to develop the main point is to cover the "why." Explain the circumstances that led to the main point.

    However you choose to elaborate upon the main point, if you have more than one elaboration to make, the subject-restriction-information technique can work well here; it shows the connection of each elaboration to the main point. For an explanation of that technique, please see Document 20, The Business Report.

- *Conclusion*: Reiterate the "what" once more and put a dramatic or memorable spin on it.

One effective variation of organizational scheme #1 is to create a "theme" speech, in which a strong theme is announced in the introduction, is clearly intertwined throughout the body, and then is dramatically reasserted in the conclusion.

For example, a speech in which an executive announces the retirement of a valued colleague might review that colleague's career and compare it to a year. It could speak of spring, summer, and autumn. It might include planting and harvesting, storms and holidays. It could close by borrowing from a Frank Sinatra song: "It was a very good year."

Organizational scheme #2

This scheme works particularly well when the "why" is just as important as the "what." Use it when you want the audience to understand why something has happened or is about to happen. Use it when you want the audience to be able to explain the main point to others.

Also use this scheme when your main point involves bad news. Just as in the bad-news business letter, this organizational scheme allows you to give the explanation for the bad news *before* you actually announce it.

This scheme consists of five parts:

- *Introduction*: Often the introduction contains only a greeting. The main point of the speech is not mentioned in this brief section. It can simply consist of something similar to "Good afternoon, and thank you for that warm reception."

- *Explanation*: The body of the speech begins here. Discuss the "why" at this time. Cover the relevant events that support the main point, even though that main point has not yet been mentioned. You are establishing a cause-effect situation. In other words, this section describes the cause, outlining all the reasons that support the main point to come. When the speaker then delivers the main point, the audience is prepared to accept it. The listeners already have heard and considered the logic that supports the main point.

- *Main Point*: The body of the speech continues, and the speaker delivers the main point, the "what." This section usually is brief. Sometimes it consists of only one sentence.

  Note again the sequence of sections: The speaker logically builds up to the main point. The main point is not mentioned until this third section of the speech.

- *Remarks*: As the body of the speech continues, the speaker develops the main point. For example, what are its consequences? What does it mean to members of the audience?

- *Conclusion*: The speaker can repeat the main point here, though such repetition often is unnecessary. The conclusion usually is concise. The speaker often appeals to the audience's emotions. Think about how many presidential speeches end with "God bless the United States of America," a powerful appeal to the emotions.

Each section in the above five-section scheme should lead logically and gracefully to the next.

Quick Tips

- Give the speech a title, even if that title is known only to you and the speaker. A title can help you stay focused on the main point.

   Consider an opening hook. Instead of "Thank you, I'm glad to be here" (or immediately after), wake up the audience with a provocative question, an outrageous statement or a short, entertaining anecdote.

- Be specific. Be innovative in how you present facts. For example: "We use four tons of paper a day. That's enough to bury this room eight feet deep—every working day of the week, every working week of the year. Eight feet deep!"

- Address the self-interest of the audience. Talk to the listeners about themselves.

- Use simple visual supplements—especially slides—if appropriate and available. Remember that what is both seen and heard often is more memorable than what is just seen or heard. If you use visual supplements, make the images extremely simple. If the listeners have to interpret images, they're not listening to the speaker.

   Be sure that you or someone tests all the materials and all the equipment in advance.

   Don't feel compelled to use visuals. In a short, well-written speech, words alone are sufficient.

- Act out the speech for yourself or a critical listener before delivering it to the speaker. Get feedback.

   Act out the speech for the speaker. Use the delivery you want her to use and ask for her feedback. This is not always possible with busy executives. And it's not always advisable if the executive is a polished speaker.

- When possible, have the speaker present the speech to you and others he trusts. Coach his delivery and get feedback from others. In some cases, the speaker may be too busy or may even be embarrassed to rehearse in front of you. If he's embarrassed, you might tactfully point out that it's better to get negative feedback from you than from the real audience.

- Be sure to have more than one copy of the speech in the room where the speaker performs the speech—just in case the main copy gets lost.

Write for the Ear, Not the Eye

The audience can't scan back up a page to clarify meaning. Therefore, consider the following:

- Have a clear beginning, middle, and end. Avoid overworked, boring transitions such as "My next point . . ." or "In conclusion. . . ."
- Keep sentences short (but vary sentence rhythms in accordance with meaning—for instance, blunt ideas should be spoken in blunt sentences; ideas designed to relax the audience should be spoken in longer, flowing sentences).
- Don't use big, pretentious words. Remember the advertising maxim "Big ideas in small words." (It can be done: Recall Hamlet's "To be or not to be—that is the question." He's discussing whether to live or die—and he's using mostly one-syllable words.)
- Avoid jargon and long, complicated sentences.
- Don't expect the audience to remember more than three key ideas.

25 The Annual Report

The Purpose

Narrowly defined, an annual report targets an organization's stockholders. It provides specifics about the organization's performance over the past year. The larger audience, however, might include stockholders, employees, investment analysts, potential investors, and government agencies.

The key to successful annual reports? Develop a clear theme, don't hide bad news, be specific, and present information in a variety of ways: articles, charts, enlarged quotations, and so on.

· Remember that your mission as business writer is to protect and promote your organization. The annual report is one of the most widely circulated documents that your organization will produce. Therefore, use it to promote your organization. The report's purpose often will be to attract investment capital and boost stock prices by portraying your organization as an attractive investment opportunity.

The Format

The format of an annual report defies concise description. Most annual reports have the format and appearance of a glossy magazine: attractive pages of type, photographs, and charts.

Often, the section titled "Management's Analysis of Financial Data" (see below) is set in smaller type than the less technical sections.

In long sections, consider using internal headlines to clarify content and increase readability.

The Content

Write clearly, using effective rhetoric, and aim for an acceptable score on the Gunning Fog Index (see Appendix B).

Focus on the long-term strategy of your organization. Discuss where you are, where you've been, and where you plan to be within the context of that strategy. Be specific. Cite precise goals and precise measurements of performance evaluation. Use numbers to show how close to your short- and long-term goals you are.

Discuss any bad news openly and show specifically how you're correcting the problems.

If possible, package all this information into a theme, either implicit or explicit, to help organize the information and keep it moving toward a clear purpose.

Organize the report, making sure to comply with any relevant laws and regulations, such as those imposed by the federal Securities and Exchange Commission, the state in which your organization is incorporated, and the stock exchanges that list your organization.

Following are the traditional sections of an annual report.

Opening Charts and Graphs That Show Basic Financial Results

These should be clearly labeled and reader-friendly.

This short section is usually just one page long, often placed on the inside front cover.

Message from the Chair

This focuses on the highlights of the year and thanks the employees, the stockholders, and other important groups. It's a personal message that should clearly reflect the chair's personality. If the report has a theme, it should be skillfully integrated here.

Within the first few sentences, this section should say how the organization did last year. Were profits up or down? Why? If profits were down, the message should specify what's being done about it.

Longer Narrative (a Feature on the Organization)

This section is similar to a magazine feature: lively, engaging, informative, and specific. This is one of your best shots at fulfilling your purpose of using the annual report to attract investments. Using smaller, inset articles or charts to highlight key information usually works well. (Not all annual reports include this section. Sometimes, the material that would go here can be included in the chair's message.)

Management's Analysis of Financial Data

These are charts with accompanying explanations that the financial personnel prepare. They'll be verified by an outside accounting agency. You probably won't do the writing, but you might help edit the prose descriptions of the charts. You will want tight writing here. Use the Gunning Fog Index (Appendix B) and good rhetoric. Casual investors may not pore over this section, but investment analysts will.

Who's Who in the Organization

Most annual reports close with information about the board of directors and other high-ranking officials in the organization. Often, this section is simply a list of names, titles, and, perhaps, photographs. Such a format can be unsatisfying for readers who want to evaluate the implementors of the long-term strategies.

Instead of such an unrevealing list, make this section of the annual report strong and detailed. State how long individuals have been with the organization and where they were before. List the individuals' specific duties that relate to the organization's goals. Perhaps quote them on their personal priorities for the organization.

Quick Tips

- Get started early. Conduct a postmortem of the previous annual report. What worked well? What didn't? Experts say that you should begin planning seven to eight months before the report's mailing date.
- Select a design that enhances the words. Hire the best designer available, one who will use photos, illustrations, and graphs to help tell the story. Some designers forget that their mission is to make the message clear and accessible. Be sure that the designer has read the current draft of the report and knows the overall theme. The design may *look* great, but it must be informative, accurate, and readable.

Writing for the Information Highway

Business writers should be familiar with the Internet, which is an international network of computers. The Internet allows you to send information from your computer and receive information from colleagues and customers. For business writers, two aspects of the Internet are most useful: electronic mail (E-mail) and the World Wide Web.

E-mail allows you to send and receive letters, memos, news releases, newsletters—any document—via your computer.

The World Wide Web is the colorful, graphics-laden area of the Internet. It is a collection of web sites that can be located and viewed with a web browser, which displays text and graphics. Each web site has an owner (such as your organization). The site generally contains information about that owner.

Each web site begins with a "home page," which is like a table of contents. A home page usually is colorful and visually interesting. It will have entries (often icons) such as "News Releases," "Who's Who," "Products and Services," "Video Tours," and so on. To reach the information in one of those areas, users simply point and click with their computer's mouse. The information may include photographs, drawings, or even video in addition to text.

The Internet is an exciting, evolving development for almost all communicators, but it's only a tool, not a strategy. It won't write documents for you. But, to paraphrase Marshall McLuhan, the medium can be the message. That is, your use of the Internet can suggest to audiences that you are eager to use every possible tool to communicate successfully with them.

E-Mail

E-Mail Basics

Keep business-related E-mail messages short.

Your E-mail screen will provide a space for the subject of your document. (The headings for most E-mail messages are similar to those of a memo.) Write an engaging, specific, accurate, short (approximately 25 characters and spaces) description. Otherwise, your document may be overwhelmed by more attractive competition.

If you're using a commercial E-mail provider that charges by the hour, don't sign on and write a long document. You're paying to write online. Instead, write your document before signing on. Have another competent editor review your E-mail document before you transmit it. Then activate your E-mail, copy your document to your E-mail screen, and send your document.

Similarly, if you receive a long document, don't remain online to read it. You're being charged to read. Instead, download the document to your hard drive, or print it. Then sign off and read at your leisure.

E-Mail Etiquette

Always include your return E-mail address.

Don't "spam" other E-mail users. Spamming means sending the same document to many different individual mailboxes, bulletin boards, and interest groups. Instead, study each recipient. Tailor the document, or at least its introduction, to that user. If it seems inappropriate for a certain recipient, don't send it.

Study bulletin boards and interest groups before posting your news releases there. This type of research is called "lurking." Get to know the style and content of the target(s) you're considering. Be sure to read the FAQ (Frequently Asked Questions) file usually available in bulletin board and interest group sites.

Internet experts discourage attaching documents to E-mail messages as separate files. Too many computer users, they say, are unable to access attached files. For best results, simply make the E-mail message itself the document. As computer literacy increases, this prohibition on attachments may ease—but, for now, don't let your document get lost in cyberspace.

E-Mail News Releases and Pitch Letters

Recent studies show that journalists prefer electronically transmitted news releases and pitch letters (as opposed to those sent through regular mail). With a perfect E-mail news release, a newspaper journalist can copy the text to the word-processing or page-design program, delete headings and footers, rewrite the headline to fit the space—and it's ready to go.

Some journalists believe it is bad form simply to assume that they prefer an E-mail submission. It's not bad form, however, to use E-mail to check on a journalist's preference. Can't find her E-mail address? Use some old-fashioned technology: the telephone.

Consider the following guidelines in using E-mail to contact journalists:

- If a reporter asks to be removed from your E-mail list, do so immediately.
- Don't include dozens of names in the "To" section of the E-mail heading. That shows journalists who else is receiving your news release.
- Because the journalist will read the release one screen at a time, the inverted-pyramid organizational scheme is essential. The most important information should come first in the news release.
- Remember the standard rules of news releases. Each release must have a relevant, interesting angle for each recipient. This may mean you will need to send out different versions of the same document.

E-Mail Newsletters

Because E-mail newsletters are typically 100 percent text, keep them short—and keep each article short. Ten to twelve lines will fill most E-mail screens. Ideally, no story should be longer than one screen. Consider stories of five to six lines to allow more than one story per screen.

If E-mail newsletter articles seem too short, use a concluding line for each that directs readers to more information—perhaps to a file in a web site that can be downloaded or to a longer article in a print newsletter.

E-Mail Memos

Treat these just like paper memos. Don't write and send them unless they must be written and sent. Don't write anything you'd be unwilling to see on the front page of the *New York Times*.

E-Mail Company Announcements

Keep these short, just like E-mail newsletter articles: 10 to 12 lines maximum. Obituaries can be longer if necessary. An obituary that's too brief can sound abrupt and heartless.

The World Wide Web

Creating a Web Site

A web site ideally should be created by an expert. When creating a web site, consider these options:

Write web site documents in HyperText Markup Language, commonly known as HTML. This language is used to program text files with typographic styles and links to other documents or web sites. Words and phrases that lead to other pages are highlighted, usually with boldface or color. Readers can point and click on those passages and move to another document. For example, clicking on **annual report** in an HTML news release would take you to the organization's annual report.

Consider including a variety of documents besides news releases and annual reports in a frequently updated web site: backgrounders, media advisories, appropriate company announcements, policy and procedure documents, business reports, newsletters, brochures, and speeches.

In addition to text documents, consider including illustrations, photographs, and audio and video material in your web site. Update your web site and its home page frequently. Once a week isn't too often.

Link your web site to other, related web sites. Your home page can help users move to those sites. For example, on your home page, a user might see the entry "Other Web Sites We Like." To see another site, she would point and click on that entry. She then could examine your list of preferred sites and visit them simply by pointing and clicking.

Using Other Web Sites (and Online Services)

Other web sites can provide material for your own documents. For example, most government agencies, political parties, corporations, libraries, and universities have web sites. Each will have information you can examine and download or print.

How can you find useful World Wide Web sites? One of the best ways to explore the web is through a site called YAHOO, which functions as a World Wide Web index. YAHOO's address is http://www.yahoo.com (no period after com).

Learn what bulletin boards and interest groups are important to audiences that you frequently address. Monitor them to enhance your knowledge of those groups.

Some commercial online services that provide Internet access will also, for a fee, act as a clipping service for you. Every day, they'll scan hundreds of online newspapers, magazines, and broadcast reports for any type of story you designate. If your organization has access to news media databases such as LEXIS/NEXIS, you can perform this service yourself.

SINGLE-ORGANIZATION EXAMPLE DOCUMENTS

Examples are often the best explanations. This unit contains examples of the documents discussed earlier—all from a single, fictional organization.

Document 1, Good-News Letter

Eclectic Catering **&** *Baked Goods*

2010 Ridglea Ave. ■ Hosea, WI 12345-6789
(555) 555-5555 ■ Fax (555) 333-4444

Aug. 1, 1996

Ms. Amy Arlaenx
Chief Executive Officer
Amy's Amazing Paper Bags, Inc.
P.O. Box 234
Denver, CO 40958

Dear Amy,

Congratulations! It is my great pleasure to tell you that Eclectic Catering & Baked Goods has named you its 1996 Supplier of the Year. The competition for this honor was most impressive, but at our July 25 meeting, the Management Council reviewed the list of finalists and resoundingly selected you as our best supplier.

Eclectic Catering & Baked Goods invites you to be its guest of honor at your awards banquet on Sept. 12, 1996, at 7 p.m. at the Royale Hotel in Denver. We'll gather for cocktails at 6 p.m. in the Casino Room. You are more than welcome to bring up to four guests. (If you'd like to bring a few more, we can certainly arrange that.) Please contact me to clarify what arrangements would be best for you.

At the banquet, Elizabeth Bennet, our president, will present you with our award—an inscribed bronze cookie—and, after the dinner, we'll invite you to speak for two or three minutes. Your speech needn't be long or elaborate; we just want another chance to cheer for you.

I hope you know what an honor it is for me to write this letter. When we were roommates 10 years ago at Palmquist University, who knew our paths would cross again at such a wonderful moment? I'm proud to claim you as a business associate and a friend.

Again, congratulations on this significant achievement in your career. Please phone me at your earliest convenience to confirm a plan.

Sincerely,

Ann Daleint

Ann Daleint
Special Events Coordinator

Document 2, Bad-News Letter

Eclectic Catering & Baked Goods

2010 Ridglea Ave. ▪ Hosea, WI 12345-6789
(555) 555-5555 ▪ Fax (555) 333-4444

Aug. 1, 1996

Mr. John Doe
123 Park Avenue
St. Paul, MN 29845

Dear Mr. Doe:

Thank you for your recent letter inquiring about a merchandising position at Eclectic Catering & Baked Goods. Your career with Bonnie's Burrito World sounds exciting, and we understand and admire your desire for new challenges.

At the moment, we have no positions available for someone with your credentials. Therefore, I'm sorry that I can't extend an invitation for you to join us at Eclectic Catering & Baked Goods. We were impressed by your résumé, however, and will keep it on file. Should an appropriate opening occur, we will contact you promptly at your home address.

Again, thank you for your interest in Eclectic Catering & Baked Goods and for your kind words about our Mimi's Best chocolate-chip cookies. Best of luck to you.

Sincerely,

Mark Markle

Mark Markle
Director of Personnel

Document 3, Sales Letter

2010 Ridglea Ave. ▪ Hosea, WI 12345-6789
(555) 555-5555 ▪ Fax (555) 333-4444

Aug. 1, 1996

Mr. George Pextriel
Special Events Coordinator
D-Man Corporation
P.O. Box 491
Salina, KS 67401

Dear Mr. Pextriel:

Caterers! They can make your job miserable. Will they be on time? Will the servers be invisible but effective? Caterers can make the difference between an event's success or failure. Who needs them? You do.

We're here to help. We're Eclectic Catering & Baked Goods, winner of *Catering* magazine's 1995 Gold Award for Superior Customer Service. Before you allow us to cater your next important event, we'll show you our Code of Excellence, which specifies the rigorously high standards we'll enforce at your event. We'll sign that code—and for every standard we fail to meet, we'll deduct 20 percent from your bill. How often do we have to do that? Less than one percent of the time.

In short, we guarantee success—or your money back.

You don't want baked goods? No problem: We serve everything from fried chicken to sashimi or bouillabaisse. And every recipe is designed to have those important attendees praising you for the best meal they've had all week.

If you want delicious, award-winning, hassle-free, guaranteed catering, call me at 1-800-555-1111. Eclectic Catering & Baked Goods is eager to be your secret weapon in the catering wars.

Tired of crossing your fingers when you hire a caterer? Eclectic Catering & Baked Goods is just a phone call away.

Sincerely,

Lynn Anslimp

Lynn Anslimp
Director of Catering

Document 5, Announcement: This is an example of a news release for the Times-Herald *newspaper in Elna, Kansas. Note the local angle in the first paragraph.*

Eclectic Catering & Baked Goods

2010 Ridglea Ave. ▪ Hosea, WI 12345-6789
(555) 555-5555 ▪ Fax (555) 333-4444

News Release

For more information, contact:
Martha Mae
    Communications Specialist
    (555) 555-5554
Terry Sharp
    Communications Specialist
    (555) 555-1234

For Immediate Release
Aug. 1, 1996

Eclectic Catering & Baked Goods wins international gold medal

Hosea, Wisc.—The International Baking Academy of Paris has awarded its Gold Medal for the World's Best Chocolate-Chip Cookie to Eclectic Catering & Baked Goods. Eclectic employs 432 workers in its Elna plant, which produces Mimi's Best, the award-winning cookie.

The Mimi's Best brand beat 231 competitors from 39 nations for the international title. In a July 30 ceremony in Paris, Pierre DeSerrte, president of the International Baking Academy, awarded the gold medal to Eclectic President Elizabeth Bennet.

– more –

Eclectic Catering -2

"There were many fine competitors but only one perfect cookie," DeSerrte said. "Mimi's Best cookies received a perfect score from each of our 12 judges."

Bennet said that several judges asked for the secret to Eclectic's baking process. "Fortunately, my French wasn't good enough to explain the process," she said, "so it remains a secret."

Bennet said that although the ingredients of Mimi's Best cookies are listed on the package, Eclectic Catering & Baked Goods keeps its special baking process confidential.

"We recently polled some of our best customers, and a majority don't want to know the secret," Bennet said. "They said they prefer a little mystery with their milk and cookies."

The gold medal is the second recent international award for Eclectic Catering & Baked Goods. In 1995, the company won the Canadian Bread Association's International Oatmeal Bread Bake-Off.

Eclectic Catering & Baked Goods was founded in 1955. The company has plants in Hosea, Wisc., and Elna, Kan.

###

Document 9, Media Advisory: This is an example of a media advisory for the Times-Herald *newspaper in Elna, Kansas. Note the local angle in the headline.*

Eclectic Catering & Baked Goods

2010 Ridglea Ave. ▪ Hosea, WI 12345-6789
(555) 555-5555 ▪ Fax (555) 333-4444

Media Advisory

For Immediate Release
Aug. 1, 1996

For more information, contact:
Martha Mae
    Communications Specialist
    (555) 555-5554
Terry Sharp
    Communications Specialist
    (555) 555-1234

Eclectic Catering & Baked Goods president to visit Elna to share international award

WHAT: Eclectic Catering & Baked Goods President Elizabeth Bennet will tour Eclectic's Elna Production Plant Monday, Aug. 12. Members of the news media are invited to speak with her at 10 a.m. in the plant's conference room.

WHY: Bennet will show each employee the gold medal that Eclectic won for its Mimi's Best chocolate-chip cookies. The award was presented by the International Baking Academy of Paris. Mimi's Best chocolate-chip cookies are baked in the Elna plant.

WHEN: Bennet will be at the Elna plant from 8 a.m. to 5 p.m.

WHERE: The Elna Production Plant is at 1400 Flora Road in Elna.

WHO: Bennet is 47. She has been president of Eclectic Catering & Baked Goods since 1985. Eclectic Catering & Baked Goods, an award-winning producer of cookies and breads, is based in Hosea, Wisc. It has production plants in both Hosea and Elna. Its 1995 sales were $1.75 billion.

###

Document 10, Pitch Letter

Eclectic Catering & *Baked Goods*

2010 Ridglea Ave. ▪ Hosea, WI 12345-6789
(555) 555-5555 ▪ Fax (555) 333-4444

Aug. 1, 1996

Mr. John Hardesty
Editor
Wisconsin Business Today
P.O. Box 143
Milwaukee, WI 19846

Dear Mr. Hardesty:

It wasn't love at first sight when Eclectic Catering & Baked Goods President Elizabeth Bennet met her husband-to-be, William Darcy. She punched him—decked him with one right hook to the jaw.

"It's so embarrassing, but I thought he was attacking one of our customers," says Bennet, who saw Darcy manhandling a customer in Eclectic's Hosea, Wisc., outlet store. "Turns out he was an undercover police officer arresting an alleged jewel thief."

Darcy recovered, arrested the alleged thief—and later proposed marriage. "Obviously, I couldn't get her off my mind," he says.

I think this stranger-than-fiction love story would be ideal for *Wisconsin Business Today* magazine. Your profiles of corporate leaders in Wisconsin have been consistently excellent, particularly the recent cover story on Martin Smith. Elizabeth Bennet is president of Wisconsin-based Eclectic Catering & Baked Goods, an award-winning producer of cookies and breads. Eclectic's 1995 sales were $1.75 billion. She'd be a natural for your leadership series.

We're offering this story exclusively to *Wisconsin Business Today*, so I'll need to know fairly soon if you're interested. I can assure you that Elizabeth Bennet will cooperate fully with your writers and photographers. She will make herself available for extensive interviews and is willing, within reasonable limits, to discuss both her personal and professional lives. If you'd like, an interview with both Elizabeth Bennet and William Darcy could be arranged. (Sorry we can't provide the alleged jewel thief; he's doing time on other charges.)

I will call on Thursday, August 8, to see if I can help you arrange interviews for a profile of Elizabeth Bennet. Thank you for your time and consideration.

Sincerely,

Frank Michaels

Frank Michaels
Public Relations Director

Document 11, Backgrounder

2010 Ridglea Ave. ▪ Hosea, WI 12345-6789
(555) 555-5555 ▪ Fax (555) 333-4444

Backgrounder

For more information, contact:
Martha Mae
Communications Specialist
(555) 555-5554
Terry Sharp
Communications Specialist
(555) 555-1234

For Immediate Release
Aug. 1, 1996

Eclectic Catering & Baked Goods'
Secret Baking Process

The ingredients of every Eclectic Catering & Baked Goods product are listed on the packaging. But the baking process? That's a secret.

"We use a process that my grandmother discovered," said Eclectic President Elizabeth Bennet. "It gives our products their light, crispy outside, but a moist, tender inside."

That baking process has helped Eclectic Catering & Baked Goods win more than a dozen national and international baked-goods competitions in the past decade.

Bennet said that Eclectic's secret baking process has prompted insatiable—and sometimes illegal—curiosity among some consumers.

"The burglar alarm in each of our plants goes off about once every three weeks," she said. "Nothing is ever missing. The police tell us that people just want to see our ovens."

"Eclectic's baking process is one of the best-kept secrets in baking," said Walter Shandy, editor of *Bake It* magazine. "I'd love to know what it is."

Eclectic Catering & Baked Goods was founded in 1955. The company has plants in Hosea, Wisc., and Elna, Kan.

###

Document 12, Fact-Sheet

2010 Ridglea Ave. ■ Hosea, WI 12345-6789
(555) 555-5555 ■ Fax (555) 333-4444

Fact Sheet

For Immediate Release
Aug. 1, 1996

For more information, contact:
Martha Mae
    Communications Specialist
    (555) 555-5554
Terry Sharp
    Communications Specialist
    (555) 555-1234

Eclectic Catering & Baked Goods wins international gold medal for chocolate-chip cookies

WHAT: Mimi's Best chocolate-chip cookies, produced by Eclectic Catering & Baked Goods of Hosea, Wisc., won a gold medal as the world's best chocolate-chip cookies.

WHO: The International Baking Academy of Paris sponsored the competition. Pierre DeSerrte, president of the academy, awarded the gold medal to Eclectic President Elizabeth Bennet.

Eclectic Catering & Baked Goods was founded in 1955. The company has plants in Hosea, Wisc., and Elna, Kan.

WHEN: The announcement and the award ceremony took place July 30.

WHERE: The ceremony was held at the headquarters of the International Baking Academy in Paris.

WHY: "There were many fine competitors but only one perfect cookie," DeSerrte said. "Mimi's Best cookies received a perfect score from each of our 12 judges."

Bennet attributed the victory to Eclectic's baking process, which is a closely guarded secret.

HOW: The Mimi's Best brand beat 231 competitors from 39 nations for the international title.

###

*Document 13, Photo Opportunity Sheet: This is an example
of a photo-opportunity sheet for the* Dallas Morning News.
Note the local angle in the headline.

2010 Ridglea Ave. ▪ Hosea, WI 12345-6789
(555) 555-5555 ▪ Fax (555) 333-4444

Photo Opportunity

For more information, contact:
Martha Mae
    Communications Specialist
    (555) 555-5554

For Immediate Release
Aug. 1, 1996

Terry Sharp
    Communications Specialist
    (555) 555-1234

100-POUND WOMAN MEETS TWO-TON ELEPHANT

What a contrast! One-hundred-pound Elizabeth Bennet, president of Eclectic Catering & Baked Goods, will hand-feed Ernie the Elephant, who weighs in at two tons. Ernie's caretakers discovered that Ernie, a popular resident of Dallas' African Adventure Theme Park, loves Mimi's Best cookies, which are produced by Eclectic. Bennet loves the cookies too—so she proposed a dessert date, and Ernie accepted.

WHAT: Elizabeth Bennet will hand-feed Ernie the Elephant 20 of Mimi's Best chocolate-chip cookies.

WHO: Eclectic Catering & Baked Goods President Elizabeth Bennet and Ernie the Elephant, a top attraction at Dallas' African Adventure Theme Park. Ernie is 10 years old. Bennet is 47. She has been president of Eclectic Catering & Baked Goods since 1985.

Eclectic Catering & Baked Goods, an award-winning producer of cookies and breads, is based in Hosea, Wisc. It has production plants in Hosea and Elna, Kan. Its 1995 sales were $1.75 billion.

WHERE: At the Water Hole in African Adventure Theme Park, 1296 LBJ Freeway, in Dallas—across the freeway from the Lone Star Mall.

WHEN: Noon, Monday, Aug. 26, 1996

HOW: News media admitted free beginning at 10:30 a.m. The Water Hole is situated outdoors, with excellent natural lighting.

###

Document 17, Memorandum

Eclectic Catering & Baked Goods

2010 Ridglea Ave. ▪ Hosea, WI 12345-6789
(555) 555-5555 ▪ Fax (555) 333-4444

Memorandum

Aug. 1, 1996

To: Barry Smith
           Purchasing Director

From: Beth Johnson   *BJ*
           Merchandising Director
           Building C, Room 4
           Ext. 3344
           bjohns@ccc.org

Subject: New-product introduction meeting

Thanks for your support at the last Management Council meeting. We're far ahead of schedule on the new-product introduction, and you deserve much of the credit.

Can we meet again before the next council meeting? Next Friday noon would work well for me again. If you're available, I'll also invite Jon Hendrix from Quality Control.

Let me know. And, again, thanks for all your hard work.

Document 18, Company Announcement

2010 Ridglea Ave. ▪ Hosea, WI 12345-6789
(555) 555-5555 ▪ Fax (555) 333-4444

News

Kenneth Mikkalsen

Associate Director of Finance Kenneth Mikkalsen died Wednesday night. He was 52 and had served the company for 12 years.

"We've lost a true friend," said Director of Finance Sid Haley. "Ken was the kind of associate everyone wanted to work with. He was brilliant, funny, hard-working, and a joy to be with. We'll miss him every day for a very long time."

Mikkalsen began his career at Eclectic Catering & Baked Goods as a Financial District Manager in 1984 and progressed steadily through positions of increasing responsibility to Associate Director of Finance. Before joining Eclectic, he served in financial positions at Worldwide Sprockets and McDaniel, Inc.

Mikkalsen is survived by his wife, Marie; a son, Henry, a student at Palmquist University; and a daughter, Jill.

Funeral arrangements are pending. In lieu of flowers, the family requests donations be made to the Heartland Cancer Foundation.

8/1/96

Document 19, Policy and Procedure Document

2010 Ridglea Ave. ▪ Hosea, WI 12345-6789
(555) 555-5555 ▪ Fax (555) 333-4444

Corporate Headquarters
Fire Evacuation Plan

When the fire alarm sounds and the emergency lights flash, please do the following:

1. **Don't panic.** The alarms are very sensitive, which allows you plenty of time for a safe evacuation.
2. **Stop what you're doing and walk calmly to the nearest stairwell.** Don't finish what you're working on, and please don't take work with you. Also, don't attempt to take the elevators because the power will be shut off.
3. **Walk down the stairs to the first floor.** Don't run down the stairs. Please assist any associates who require help. Again, you should have plenty of time, and the stairwells are fire resistant.
4. **Use the south exits at the bottom of the stairwells.** For your own protection, do not attempt to enter the first-floor lobby.
5. **Gather in the southernmost part of the south courtyard.** Please await further instructions there.

Special instructions for Floor Monitors:

- When a fire alarm sounds, calmly ensure that all employees exit to the stairwells.
- Remind employees, as needed, of the five points listed above.
- Check that all offices and restrooms on your floor are vacated.
- Use the stairwells to exit to the south courtyard.
- Please make sure that all stairwell doors are closed.

Revised: June 1, 1996

APPENDICES

The ACT Agenda: An Editing and Proofreading System

The ACT Agenda helps you edit and proofread business documents. Using it, you can deliver a document that is

- error-free
- thorough
- well-organized
- persuasive
- timely

The ACT Agenda has three stages: ACT One, ACT Two, and ACT Three. Each stage has three steps—and the initial letters of each stage's three steps spell ACT.

This memory trick can help you remember the nine steps of the ACT Agenda. Please read on; this *will* become clear.

Ideally, the ACT Agenda's nine steps should be memorized. When you periodically review them as your document progresses, you'll be rewarded with something that's too rare—an excellent business document. The next sections describe each of the three ACTs in greater detail.

The ACT Agenda: ACT One

Accurate

- Double-check every supposed fact in the final draft: names and spellings (of people, programs, and so on), job titles, arithmetic, quotations, and the like.
- In your copy of the final draft, place a check mark over each fact as you verify it. (These check marks needn't be in the copy you deliver to your client or your manager.) This process allows you to keep track of what you've verified and what you haven't.

ACT ONE

The three steps of ACT One help you create a document that is

- Accurate
- Correct
- Thorough

These basics form ACT One—the ground-level stage. Accurate data, correct grammar, and thorough coverage are fundamental to any successful document. ACT One ensures the fundamentals.

ACT TWO

ACT Two focuses on the finer points—that is, on making the document

- Attractive
- Coherent
- Thematic

Attractive, in this case, doesn't mean pretty. It means "Is the writing persuasive? Does it attract—not repel—the reader?"

Coherent means "Do the different parts of the document fit together logically and gracefully?"

Thematic means "Does everything in the document support a well-defined purpose?"

ACT THREE

ACT Three goes beyond the text of the document. ACT Three assumes that the text is now magnificent, so it helps you avoid pitfalls as you deliver the document to the client or to your manager.

ACT Three helps you ensure that your work is

- Assisted
- Confirmed
- Timely

Assisted work involves team-produced documents. Is everyone's work up to your standards?

Confirmed work has been approved by your managers and, if necessary, by the legal department.

Timely work makes its deadline.

- Proceed one sentence at a time. Don't be overwhelmed by the entire document. Begin with the first sentence, verify the supposed facts, if any, and then move to the second sentence.
- Remember that accuracy alone sometimes isn't enough. Facts should appear in the proper context. For example, a newsletter article praising a filled quota should include the fact that the quota had been lowered because it couldn't be filled earlier. Always remember: Good ethics means good business.

Correct

- Use flawless grammar, including spelling and punctuation. Mastering grammar is a never-ending challenge, so resign yourself to the agony and ecstasy of being a perpetual student. A knowledge of grammar also allows you to explain the logic of your word choice and sentence structure to others. If you need help, Strunk and White's *The Elements of Style* is a good place to start.
- Keep a written list of your grammatical weaknesses (a personal Hall of Shame), including a separate list of words you have misspelled or frequently look up. Review those lists often. Proofread for those particular errors.
- Proofread backward one sentence (not one word) at a time. That is, carefully review the document's last sentence for good grammar, then the second-to-last sentence, and so on. This breaks up the narrative flow and lets you focus on each sentence. (Don't combine this process with the separate fact-checking step. That's asking too much of yourself, and the document could suffer.)
- Ensure that everyone on your business-writing team has a copy of and is using the same stylebook (the *Associated Press Stylebook* works well) and the same dictionary.
- Be diplomatic in correcting others' grammar. A first-rate knowledge of grammar and a keen sense of diplomacy will help make you an indispensable, promotable member of any business-writing team.

Thorough

- Before, during, and after writing, review the document's audience and purpose. Don't simply pay lip service to this step. Do it painstakingly, because knowledge of audience and purpose will tell you how thorough the document should be.

  Before creating a business document, many companies use a prepared form on which you specify audience and purpose. Concise, specific descriptions of audience and purpose can help you determine not only content but also organization, tone, and word choice.

A key question to ask yourself is "What is the self-interest of the audience in this situation?"

- Consider writing, for your own use, concise, specific, descriptions of audience and purpose. See if you can state the document's purpose in one sentence.
- Challenge each draft in terms of who, what, when, where, why, and how. Perhaps not each of these will apply to your document—but consider each, and thoroughly develop those that are relevant.
- Beware of being overly thorough. Too many details can be as annoying as too few. Deliver only those that are necessary and/or interesting.

The ACT Agenda: ACT Two

Attractive

This area, more than any other, separates the gifted business writer from the average business writer. The outline of Attractive appears here—but please see Unit One: Rhetoric and Business Writing for specific details on how to produce writing that attracts the reader.

- Strive for brevity, courtesy, effective word choice, and effective word order.
- Avoid stereotypical, discriminatory, or insulting language in the following areas: age, sex, disability, race, religion, and national origin.
- Avoid "bizspeak" (that is, inflated, pompous, and jargonish words that sound important).
- Watch out for inappropriate timing. For example, during the U.S. bombing raids on Iraq in January 1991, Foote, Cone, & Belding Communications considered stopping one of its ad campaigns. The slogan of the campaign, for Tombstone Pizza, was "What do you want on your tombstone?"
- Avoid "you and us" constructions. For example, "When you joined our company, you . . ." can make readers feel that they're not part of the team.
- Stay away from the pronouns *I* and *you* when delivering bad news. For example, "I found 12 errors in your document." Instead, use "This document contained 12 errors. Please review and correct."

Coherent

Don't confuse this word with clear or comprehensible. Coherent, in a nutshell, means that all the parts fit together logically and gracefully.

- Ask yourself: Is the document well organized? Is the arrangement of the parts logical? Is there a reason for the chosen order?

- Now ask yourself: Does the document flow well? Are the transitions from point to point logical and smooth? Does sentence lead effectively to sentence? Paragraph to paragraph? Section to section?

- When appropriate, consider the value of transitional words (*however, therefore, also,* and so on).

- When appropriate, seek smooth transitions from paragraph to paragraph. At this level, transitional devices usually occur in the first sentence of the new paragraph. A transitional first sentence can do two things: (1) clarify the connection to the previous paragraph or to the purpose of the document and (2) announce the subject of the new paragraph. Thus, you don't lose readers as they pause to wonder about the connection.

- Recall that many other devices and techniques can support coherency: a table of contents, main headlines and internal headlines, marginal "descriptors" (descriptive notes placed in the margins that describe the content of the text next to them), and bullets, such as the dots used on this page.

Thematic

- State concisely the specific purpose of your document—ideally, in one tight sentence. (This sentence need not appear in your document.) Be sure to do this; again, never pay only lip service to purpose.

- Be sure that everything in the document supports your clearly defined purpose.

- Examine all passages that don't support the purpose. Either they don't belong, or you should redefine the purpose to include them.

- Challenge all first-person singular pronouns (the *I*'s and *me*'s). Are they absolutely necessary? When you write, "I know this plan will work," you ask your audience to focus on two things: you (you've referred to yourself) and the plan (which will work). The focus on you, usually, is unnecessary. You don't want readers to have double vision. You want their attention to be solely on the fact that the plan will work.

- In short, strive for what Edgar Allan Poe, a master of the short story, called "totality." Poe believed that a good composition should have a clear purpose and that everything in that composition should support that purpose.

The ACT Agenda: ACT Three

Assisted

- Keep informed of the progress, or lack thereof, of all associates assisting you with the document. Don't let your hard work be ruined by someone else's failure.

- If you're in charge of the team creating the document, establish each associate's task, set clear and reasonable deadlines, and hold frequent meetings or have informal daily contact. Your continued interest will create incentive for others to perform well. They won't want to face you every day with admissions of failure.

- If you're not in charge of the document team, don't run to the team leader to report a colleague's poor performance or missed deadlines. If possible, suggest that the team leader hold a progress-review meeting.

- Be diplomatic as you monitor others' progress. A friendly, competent team player is more valuable to an organization than a sullen, unpopular genius.

Confirmed

- Recall that your document usually will be reviewed at several levels—including, sometimes, a legal department—before it is released to an audience. Do your best work, because many high-ranking managers will be examining it.

- Be sure that the document's production schedule includes time for the review process. If you're in charge of this process, know who and where the reviewers are and know the order of review. Will all reviewers see the document simultaneously? Or will they see it one at a time with requested revisions made between each transfer? (If there's time, this second method can be effective—especially if you let the current reviewer know who has already approved the document.)

- Attach to each document a polite memo asking the reviewer to examine the document. Include a diplomatically expressed deadline for the reviewer's response, and indicate that silence on his part will be taken to mean that the document is fine. (If the document draft is going to a client outside your organization, a letter would be more appropriate than a memo.)

- Keep a record of the review process: who should see the document, who has seen it, when they received it, what their deadlines were, and when they returned the document.

- During this involved process, do your best to prevent reviewers from weakening the document. Some reviewers may try to inject pompous jargon, which will harm readability. Some reviewers may try to remove potentially controversial information that the audience ought to know. This could harm credibility. Remember: Good ethics means good business.

- Be prepared, however, to graciously accept reasonable changes. Be a team player.

Timely

- Don't miss deadlines. Don't miss deadlines. Don't miss deadlines. If deadlines are vague, clarify them. If you are going to miss a deadline, communicate that fact as soon as possible. Don't wait until the due date to say, "Sorry . . ."

- Devise a calendar with periodic deadline reminders. (For example, an entry for one day might be "Document X due in one week.") Large wall-chart calendars can display several months at a glance.

- Don't forget to allow time for the nonwriting part of the creative process: brainstorming, reviewing, printing, binding, distributing, and so on.

- Be aware of the time lapse between writing and publication. If you are describing an event that hasn't yet taken place *but* will have occurred by the publication date, be sure to write your document in the past tense.

APPENDIX B

THE GUNNING FOG INDEX

The Gunning Fog Index evaluates the readability of a written passage. Similar systems exist, but the Gunning Fog Index is easy to use and easy to explain to clients. It has become an industry standard.

Consistent use of concise, graceful sentences and clear, direct language will help ensure an acceptable score on the Gunning Fog Index.

Using the Index

1. In a two- or three-paragraph stretch of text, determine the average number of words per sentence.
2. In the same passage, mark off the first 100 words. In that group, how many words of three or more syllables are there? *Don't* count the following:
   - names of people, organizations, and so on
   - verbs with -ed or -es endings when that suffix creates a third syllable
   - easily recognizable compound words such as *marketplace*
3. Add the average sentence length to the number of long words. Multiply the sum by 0.4.
4. The score reveals the school grade level of the prose. For example, an 8 suggests the prose is understandable to eighth graders. Generally, business documents should score in the 8 to 12 range, but the ideal score depends upon the nature of the audience.
5. Consider testing three or four passages to ensure that your original Gunning Fog score is representative of the document.

Adapted from *The Technique of Clear Writing,* by Robert Gunning (New York: McGraw-Hill, 1952.)

APPENDIX C

WRITING A RÉSUMÉ AND COVER LETTER

THE RÉSUMÉ

A résumé is a one-page summary of your education, professional experience, and related work experience. It can include information on honors you have achieved and activities to which you devote or have devoted time. It is sent to potential employers, often with a cover letter, a list of references, and some work samples, if applicable.

Common Questions About Résumés

What should be the goal of my résumé?

To show that you're concise, well-organized, specific, versatile, and professionally experienced—and to show that you get along well with others (membership in professional associations, charitable organizations, and the like can help you achieve the last goal).

What information should my résumé include?

Name; address (if you're a college student, include school and permanent addresses); phone number(s); education; and experience. Options are skills (foreign language, computer programs, and so on), activities, and honors.

At the top of your résumé where you list your name, address(es), and phone number(s), consider including your E-mail address and personal web site on the Internet, if you have them.

Is there one proper résumé format?

No. There are several. Résumé "how-to" books can show you different approaches. Most of these wisely recommend that you keep your résumé to one page. One caution: Don't try to be excessively innovative, certainly not to the point where your résumé is hard to read.

Should I include a "Personal Objective" or
"Career Objective" near the top?

There's nothing wrong with including an objective, but conveying that information is the duty of your résumé cover letter. If you do include a career objective in your résumé, keep it very short. Also, don't list what *you* hope to gain; that can suggest to employers that you're self-centered and not a team player.

Should I list references on my résumé?

It's unlikely that there will be enough room on your résumé to include references. Send your references on a separate sheet of paper labeled *References*. Include your own name, address(es), and phone number(s) on that sheet. Don't staple it to your résumé. (See additional guidelines under "The References Sheet" below.)

Does my résumé have to be on plain white paper?

No, but avoid nontraditional colors and designs that may suggest a lack of professionalism. A conservative approach is often best. In résumés, most employers prefer good writing and impressive achievements to unusual colors or distracting designs.

Can I use a typewriter for my résumé?

No. Use a word processor and a high quality laser printer.

Tips for College Students or Recent Graduates

Should I include my grade point average?

Potential employers generally expect to see it, but it's not required. If you include it, show it as a ratio: 3.8/4.0.

Should I include jobs I've had that have little relationship
to the potential position?

Absolutely, but include only those jobs you've had since graduating from high school. Such jobs show work ethic, versatility, and the ability to get along with others. Listing good professional jobs or internships is essential, but employers realize that you've been a student for the past several years. They don't expect to see a long list of professional jobs. They will, however, be looking for a strong work ethic.

Should I include jobs and honors from high school?

No. Some employers have the perception, fair or not, that high school students are not adults. Employers are interested in your achievements as an adult.

Résumé Guidelines

When describing job duties, lead with powerful, specific action verbs: *wrote, edited, coordinated, managed, developed,* and so on. Be consistent. Don't suddenly switch from a powerful, specific verb to an adjective such as *Responsible for* . . .

List jobs chronologically, starting with the most recent. Show the month and year of all start and stop dates.

If you're no longer performing a listed job, be sure that those powerful, specific verbs are in past tense. If you're still doing the job, the verbs should be in present tense.

Work hard to think of the legitimate communications value of seemingly non-career-related jobs. For example, if you were a sales clerk, you might say that you *"represented the company to approximately 120 customers a day."* Do not stretch the truth.

Strive to keep the résumé to one page.

Make no mistakes. None. Proofread the résumé forward and backward. Then put it aside, come back to it fresh, and proofread it again. Have friends proofread it. Mistakes simply are unacceptable. This applies to your cover letter as well.

Don't staple anything to your one-page résumé. Paper-clip your cover letter, references, and any work samples to it. The traditional order is cover letter, résumé, references, and work samples.

The color of the résumé paper doesn't have to match that of the cover letter, but avoid an unattractive clash.

The References Sheet

List three to four professional associates (particularly current or past supervisors) or college professors from courses you recently completed.

Be certain that you've asked these individuals to serve as references. Provide them with a copy of your résumé.

At the top of your references sheet, duplicate the top of your résumé: your name, address(es), phone numbers, and, perhaps, E-mail address and personal web site on the Internet.

Under those headings, in bold type, place the word *References.* Below that, list your references.

List this information for each reference:

Name
Title
Employer
Business street address
City, State ZIP
Business phone number
Business E-mail address, if applicable

THE COVER LETTER (AND WHAT TO DO AFTER IT SUCCEEDS)

Target

Create a list of organizations you'd like to work for. Consider elements such as profession, region, prestige, and salary. Current business magazines, city directories, and books such as *The 100 Best Companies to Work for in America* can help. Ask a reference librarian to help direct you in your search for information.

Research

Researching business organizations has never been easier. Visit the library nearest you and ask the librarian what computerized business databases—both online and on disk—are available. Chances are good that you'll learn more than just address, officers, and annual profits. You'll learn why the organizations have been in the news in recent months. You'll learn what local papers as well as the *Wall Street Journal* or *Business Week* say about them.

The Business Periodicals Index (a book published in monthly and annual installments) also can direct you to articles about your chosen organizations.

Finally, keep up with publications such as *Business Week*, *Fortune*, *Forbes*, and the *Wall Street Journal*.

Write the Letter

Write a personal—not a form—letter on good cotton-fiber paper, not erasable bond. Use a laser printer. Keep it to one page.

Use the following headings:

Your street address
City, State ZIP
The date

Mr. or Ms. Recipient's First and Last Name
Recipient's title
Recipient's organization
Street address
City, State ZIP

Dear Mr. or Ms. Last Name:

Begin by saying why you're writing and who you are. For example:

Please consider this letter to be my application for a position as an account manager at Jones & Jones. This May I will receive a bachelor of science degree, with honors, in journalism from the University of Kansas. I'd like to continue to develop my public relations skills with an industry leader. That's why I want to work for Jones & Jones. (Note the importance of closing emphasis in this paragraph.)

In the second paragraph, demonstrate that this isn't just a form letter. Show that your specific knowledge of the organization makes you eager to work there:

Why Jones & Jones? Because of the handling of the Fat Burger account that not only won a Bronze Quill award but also helped set record profits for that restaurant. Because of 10 new clients and eight public service awards in the past nine months. Because I know I can find both challenges and rewards in a company that . . .

This paragraph will grab the recipient's attention. She's used to receiving form-letter job requests. Your letter will stand out because you:

- didn't write a form letter
- worked harder than other job applicants
- used a smarter approach than other job applicants
- showed that you really do want to work for this particular organization
- flattered the recipient by showing such specific, well-informed interest in her organization
- eased the recipient's fears about hiring you. You're clearly smart and hard-working. You'll help her gain a reputation for bringing good employees into the organization.

In the third paragraph, sell yourself. Be specific about your accomplishments and what you can bring to the organization. Name former employers and particular successes. Create a strong visual image of yourself performing specific tasks. It's fine to repeat parts of your résumé here:

I believe that I have the skills to be a part of Jones & Jones' success story. As I hope you'll see on my résumé, I . . . .

In the fourth and final paragraph, close by showing initiative:

I will call next week to see if we can schedule an interview. Until then, thank you very much for your time and your consideration.

Sincerely,
(Be sure to sign the letter!)

Your typed name

The final paragraph shows polite aggressiveness, a good quality in a prospective employee. You're not saying, *I hope to hear from you at your earliest convenience.* You're trying to make something happen by calling the recipient.

You may wish to send this letter to more than one person at the organization. If so, type

cc: name
       name

at the bottom of the letter. Address each letter to each new recipient, however. Don't just send them a copy of the letter addressed to the original recipient.

Do your best to avoid mechanical, stilted writing. Strive for a tone that shows you are an intelligent, articulate, witty, ambitious job seeker.

Rewrite and Proofread

As with your résumé, put the letter aside for at least 24 hours and come back to it fresh. Where does it sound awkward? Rewrite those passages. Experiment. Find a voice that sounds like you at your best.

Proofread the letter backward. Check your signature and the words around it, and then examine each sentence, starting with the last one. Look up the spelling of every word of which you're not absolutely certain. Double-check all the information you've included about the organization, including the spelling of the organization's name and the recipient's name. *This is a crucial step. There can be no mistakes.*

Attach Your Résumé

Attach, with a paper clip, your one-page, laser-printed résumé.

Prepare the Envelope

Don't hand-letter the envelope. Use a word processor and a good printer or a good typewriter. Include your full return address. Don't list the person's title on the envelope. Simply write

Mr. or Ms. Recipient's First and Last Name
Recipient's organization
Street address or P.O. box
City, State ZIP

Call to Schedule the Interview

Have a set speech ready. Remind the recipient of your letter and ask if an interview is possible. If you can't get past the secretary, settle for asking for the letter recipient to return your call. Be polite! The secretary's opinion of you can be a key element in whether or not you'll be hired.

Prepare for the Interview

Review potential questions. What are your strengths? Your weaknesses? Why do you want to work for the organization? What's the most rewarding thing you've ever done? What are your pet peeves? Who are your heroes? Where do you want to be in 10 years? Describe a recent situation in which you persuaded somebody to do something.

Be sure to learn and memorize even more information about the organization than your letter contained. Work that information gracefully into your answers.

Be ready with questions of your own that incorporate your knowledge of the organization.

Have a well-organized, diverse, professional-looking portfolio of your work. Organizing it by subject (with divider tabs) can be best—that is, a section for news releases, a section for newsletter articles, and so on. An opening table of contents (no need to list page numbers) can show the diversity of the portfolio. Often, the first page of your portfolio is your résumé.

Dress for the Interview

Select clothing in which you feel professional and comfortable.

Control the Interview

Remember your agenda: You're there to prove that you know this organization well and that you have specific job skills that this organization can use.

Be calm and bright. Give a firm handshake if a hand is offered. Answer the questions, and, when possible, develop your answers based on your knowledge of the organization and your specific skills. Work in information about the organization. Steer answers toward your strengths and accomplishments. *Maintain eye contact.* Have questions ready should the interviewer ask, "What questions do you have about us?"

Write a Follow-up Letter(s)

Immediately after the interview, send a brief, typed thank-you letter in which you thank the recipient for the interview, mention something specific you appreciated learning during the interview (for example, some impressive information about the organization) and gracefully ask for the job.

If you interviewed with more than one person at the organization, send each person an individual letter. Vary your wording so the letters are not duplicates.

If the secretary was particularly useful, be sure to write him or her a thank-you letter as well. Courtesy and professionalism are appreciated and remembered.

Write a thank-you letter to anyone else who helped you get the interview, even if that individual isn't an employee of the organization. For example, you may want to thank your references.

APPENDIX D

RECOMMENDED RESOURCES

Works on Grammar and Style

The Associated Press Stylebook and Libel Manual, 30th edn. (New York: The Associated Press, 1995).
> *The most widely used stylebook for the news media. Includes comprehensive libel and copyright guidelines.*

Lanham, Richard. *Revising Business Prose*, 3rd edn. (New York: Macmillan, 1992).
> *Includes Lanham's highly effective system for removing deadwood from business writing.*

Orwell, George. "Politics and the English Language" in *Shooting an Elephant and Other Essays* (New York: Harcourt Brace Jovanovich, 1950). Online at http://kuhttp.cc.ukans.edu/carrie/carrie_main.html.
> *An entertaining analysis of uncluttered, engaging writing. Ends with Orwell's six rules for readable writing, including "Never use a metaphor, simile, or other figure of speech which you are used to seeing in print" and "If it is possible to cut a word out, always cut it out."*

Strunk, William, and White, E.B. *The Elements of Style*, 3rd edn. (New York: Macmillan, 1979).
> *The best short guide to clear, concise, correct writing.*

Works on Public Relations Writing

Bivins, Thomas. *Handbook for Public Relations Writing*, 3rd edn. (Lincolnwood, IL: NTC Business Books, 1995).
> *A comprehensive public-relations writing textbook. Includes chapters on advertising and working with printers.*

Dodd, Julie; Keller, Ken; Plumley, Joe; Woods, Gail Baker; Smeyak, Paul; and Walsh-Childers, Kim. *Mass Media Writing: An Introduction.* (Scottsdale, AZ: Gorsuch Scarisbrick, Publishers, 1997).
> *An introduction to all aspects of mass media writing, including advertising, public relations, radio, television, news, and editorial.*

Levine, Michael. *Guerrilla PR: How You Can Wage an Effective Publicity Campaign . . . Without Going Broke* (New York: HarperBusiness, 1993).
   An entertaining, nonacademic guide to publicity. Strong blend of strategies and examples.

Newsom, Douglas, and Carrell, Bob. *Public Relations Writing: Form and Style*, 4th edn. (Belmont, CA: Wadsworth, 1995).
   A comprehensive public relations writing textbook. Includes sections on writing for small audiences, special audiences, and the mass media.

Public Relations Society of America. *Public Relations Tactics.* (Public Relations Society of America, 33 Irving Place, New York, NY 10003–2376).
   Monthly newsletter that does an excellent job of reviewing the evolving use of the Internet by business communicators.

Smith, Ronald D. *Becoming a Public Relations Writer: A Writing Process Workbook for the Profession* (New York: HarperCollins, 1996).
   A comprehensive public relations writing textbook. Contains an excellent chapter on news-release writing. Includes a chapter on direct-mail appeals.

Tucker, Kerry; Derelian, Doris; and Rouner, Donna. *Public Relations Writing: An Issue-Driven Approach*, 2nd edn. (Englewood Cliffs, N.J.: Prentice Hall, 1994).
   Excellent information on how to analyze audiences and craft appropriate messages. Primary focus is on media-relations documents. Includes chapters on getting a first job and organizing special events and news conferences.

Wilcox, Dennis L., and Nolte, Lawrence W. *Public Relations Writing and Media Techniques*, 2nd edn. (New York: HarperCollins, 1995).
   A comprehensive public relations writing textbook. Includes a chapter on letters, proposals, and reports. Also includes chapters on photographs and illustrations, advertising, and meeting and event preparation.

Works on Business Writing

Baugh, L. Sue; Fryar, Maridell; and Thomas, David. *Handbook for Business Writing* (Lincolnwood, IL: NTC Business Books, 1994).
   Covers business writing documents such as letters, memos, and reports but also includes a section on news releases.

Bruce, Harry J.; Hirst, Russel K.; and Keene, Michael L. *A Short Guide to Business Writing* (Englewood Cliffs, N.J.: Prentice Hall, 1995).
  Includes detailed discussion of reports and speeches. Includes brief discussions of letters, memos, résumés, and personal portfolios.

Coxford, Lola, M. *Résumé Writing Made Easy*, 5th edn. (Scottsdale, AZ: Gorsuch Scarisbrick, Publishers, 1995).
  A step-by-step guide of how to sell yourself on paper. Includes sample résumés for more than 120 job categories.

Lesikar, Raymond V., and Pettit, John D. Jr. *Report Writing for Business*, 9th edn. (Homewood, IL: Irwin, 1995).
  Focuses exclusively and comprehensively on business reports. Includes chapters on cross-cultural communication, oral reports, and new research tools.

Lesikar, Raymond V.; Pettit, John D. Jr.; and Flatley, Marie E. *Lesikar's Basic Business Communication*, 7th edn. (Homewood, IL: Irwin, 1996).
  A standard on college campuses. Particularly good analyses and examples of business letters. Includes chapters on technology, cross-cultural communication, and research methods.

Works on Web Sites and HyperText Markup Language (HTML)

Lemay, Laura. *Teach Yourself Web Publishing with HTML in a Week* (Indianapolis: Sams Publishing, 1995).
  A solid introduction to HTML.

National Center for Supercomputing Applications (NCSA). *A Beginner's Guide to HTML.* Online at http://www.ncsa.uiuc.edu/General/Internet/www/HTMLPrimer.html.
  One of the best guides to creating HyperText Markup Language documents. Includes a glossary and clear examples.

Sanders, Tony. *HTML Bad Style Page.* Online at http://www.earth.com/bad-style.
  An entertaining, understandable list of HTML taboos. Includes links to other good HTML tutorials.

Media Directories

Bacon's Media Directories (Chicago: Bacon's Information Inc.).
A reliable annual directory of newspapers, magazines, radio stations, and television stations. Includes editors' names, titles, phone numbers, and fax numbers.

Working Press of the Nation Media Directories (New Providence, N.J.).
Like the Bacon's directory, a reliable annual directory of newspapers, magazines, radio stations, and television stations. Includes editors' names, titles, phone numbers, and fax numbers.

INDEX